Paths to Salvation

Other Books of Interest from St. Augustine's Press

George William Rutler, *Principalities and Powers: Spiritual Combat 1942–1943*

Jeffrey J. Langan, *The French Revolution Confronts Pius VI*

Ernest A. Fortin, *Christianity and Philosophical Culture in the Fifth Century: The Controversy about the Human Soul in the West*

Florent Gaboriau, *The Converstion of Edith Stein*

Ralph McInerny, *The Defamation of Pius XII*

Roger Scruton, *The Politics of Culture and Other Essays*

Roger Scruton, *The Meaning of Conservatism*

Roger Scruton, *An Intelligent Person's Guide to Modern Culture*

Rémi Brague, *The Legitimacy of the Human*

Rémi Brague, *Moderately Modern*

Christopher Wolfe (editor), *The Concept of Social Justice*

Ellis Sandoz, *The Politics of Truth and Other Untimely Essays: The Crisis of Civic Consciousness*

Ellis Sandoz, *Give Me Liberty*

Daniel J. Mahoney, *The Other Solzhenitsyn: Telling the Truth about a Misunderstood Writer and Thinker*

Peter Kreeft, *Socrates' Children: The 100 Greatest Philosophers*

Gerhart Niemeyer, *Between Nothingness and Paradise*

Gerhart Niemeyer, *The Loss and Recovery of Truth*

Pierre Manent, *Seeing Things Politically: Interviews with Benedicte Delorme-Montini*

Albert Camus, *Christian Metaphysics and Neoplatonism*

Barry Cooper, *Consciousness and Politics*

Montgomery C. Erfourth, *A Guide to Understanding Eric Voegelin's Political Reality*

Josef Pieper, *Enthusiasm and Divine Madness*

Josef Pieper, *Don't Worry about Socrates*

Paths to Salvation:
The National Socialist Religion

Klaus Vondung

Translated by William Petropulos

St. Augustine's Press
South Bend, Indiana

Manufactured in the United States of America.

1 2 3 4 5 6 25 24 23 22 21 20 19

Library of Congress Control Number: 2019936070

Originally published in Germany. *Deutsche Wege zur Erlösung: Formen des Religiösen im Nationalsozialismus*. Wilhelm Fink Verlag, München 2013

∞ The paper used in this publication meets the minimum requirements of the American National Standard for Information Sciences - Permanence of Paper for Printed Materials, ANSI Z39.48-1984.

St. Augustine's Press
www.staugustine.net

CONTENTS

In silence the millions bowed to him. Redeemed.

Gerhard Schumann, *Die Lieder vom Reich*

INTRODUCTION

"First they behave like swine and then they want to be redeemed." With these words Gottfried Benn criticized not only the leaders of the Third Reich but the people who had acclaimed them. The sentence is from his essay, "Concerning History," written in the early 1940s and at first only intended for his desk drawer.[1] Yet in 1933 Gottfried Benn was also among those who had acclaimed the "new" National Socialist State. Klaus Mann, in a letter from his exile in Sanary-sur-mer in southern France, asked Benn how an intellectual and writer of distinction could possibly bring himself to embrace National Socialism.[2] And Benn replied sharply, taunting the exiled writers in a radio broadcast and in an open letter: "It's high time you people on your Latin sea [Karl Kraus conjectured that this phrase meant 'you in your inferior landscape'[3]] begin to realize that what is at stake is not a form of government but a new vision of the birth of man."[4] Here Benn betrayed not only the literary avant-garde, whose views he had once shared, but his own work up to this time: "The age of art is gone forever!"[5] With this statement Benn took leave of his expressionist past and indeed of the art epoch of the last five hundred years. Perhaps he, too, hoped for something like redemption from the upheaval that in his view was not about forms of government but perhaps "the last great idea of the white race itself and quite probably one of the greatest actualizations of the world spirit ever."[6]

1 Gottfried Benn, *Sämtliche Werke. Stuttgarter Ausgabe*, ed. Gerhard Schuster. vol. 4, Prose 2. (Stuttgart: Klett-Cotta, 1989), 292. The essay "Zum Thema Geschichte" was written before 1943, and the earliest notes may date back to 1937.

2 Ibid., 510–512.

3 Karl Kraus, *Die Dritte Walpurgisnacht* (Munich: Kösel, 1952), 70. The text was originally written for an issue of the *Fackel* ("Warum die Fackel nicht erscheint," nr. 890–905, end of July 1934) where it appeared without the passages on Benn.

4 Benn, "Antwort an die literarischen Emigranten," in *Sämtliche Werke* vol. 4, 27.

5 Benn, "Expressionismus," in ibid., 87.

6 Benn, "Antwort an die literarischen Emigranten," in ibid., 27.

Still, it did not take long for Benn to realize his error. In August 1934 he wrote to Ina Seidel: "It's a horrible tragedy! Gradually the whole thing begins to look like a second-rate-theater that continually announces *Faust* but whose cast is only up to staging *Husarenfieber.*[7] How wonderful it began and how tawdry it has become."[8] Maybe Benn developed a sharp eye for mendacious claims and "ham-acting" because for awhile he, too, had been seduced by hopes of redemption. In "Concerning History" he makes a salient observation: "Particularly suspicious is the idea of redemption that runs through their musical and stage dramas: *Tannhäuser* and its variations, *The Flying Dutchman*, *Parsifal*, not *Faust* but Faustian motifs; [...] they all have their 'urgings,' which is Faustian, and then they want to be redeemed."[9]

Indeed, both before and after 1933 the National Socialists spoke often of the longing for redemption. In 1924 Joseph Goebbels confided to his diary: "Out of the despair and leaden skepticism of these last years I have managed to find faith again in the nation and the German spirit. I feel strong now and more ardently than ever anticipate redemption."[10] At the end of the First World War and during the troubled years that followed, a widespread longing emerged for a great leader who would lift the nation's spirit and banish the evils that plagued it. Ulrich Linse has shown that after 1918 a number of such redeemer figures were underway in political, social, and spiritual subcultures: "barefoot prophets" and "inflation saints." "The existence of the inflation saints reveals how people who experience a profound crisis of meaning in their lives can develop such an attitude of expectation and look to heroic redeemer figures for the answers to their fears. And the appearance of the inflation saints also demonstrates that the messianic Hitler was by no means an isolated phenomenon."[11] However, in

7 Gustav Kadelburg and Richard Skowronnek, *Husarenfieber* (1926). Filmed in 1925.

8 Gottfried Benn, *Ausgewählte Briefe,* with an Afterword by Max Rychner (Wiesbaden: Limes-Verlag, 1957), 58.

9 Benn, *Sämtliche Werke*, vol. 4, Prose 2, 292.

10 Elke Fröhlich, ed., *Die Tagebücher von Joseph Goebbels*, Part 1, vol. 1/I (Munich: Saur, 1987), 135. (May 16, 1924).

11 Ulrich Linse, *Barfüßige Propheten. Erlöser der zwanziger Jahre* (Berlin: Siedler, 1983), 40. Cf. Peter Longerich, *Goebbels. Biographie* (Munich: Siedler, 2010), 58.

contrast to the inflation saints, Hitler succeeded in overcoming the sectarian image and gained the position of a political leader who promised to redeem the nation. Writers in particular lent eloquence to these hopes. For example, in "The German Prayer" the young Herbert Böhme paid homage to the leader:

> You stride among the people as its redeemer
> Because you are possessed by faith.[12]

And Gerhard Schumann, in his *Songs of the Reich*, purportedly written in 1930, hoped that Hitler's coming to power would bring redemption, an act that he saw in terms of Jesus' night of agony on the Mount of Olives:

> Night came. One stood and struggled.
> And blood flowed from the eyes that watching
> Died in terror at the horror
> That rose from the valleys to the mountain peak.
>
> Desperate cries broke, shrill and lost.
> With a final grasp despair clutched into the void.
> He rose up straight, trembling under the burden,
> Until the command forced him to his knees.
>
> But then as he rose again, the elect's
> Burning halo adorned his brow and descending
> He carried the flaming torch into the night.
>
> In silence the millions bowed to him.
> Redeemed. The sky blazed pale morning.
> The sun grew and with the sun grew the Reich.[13]

12 Herbert Böhme, *Das Deutsche Gebet* (Munich: Eher, 1936), 14 ["vom Glauben ganz besessen"].

13 Gerhard Schumann, *Die Lieder vom Reich* (Munich: Langen and Müller, 1935), 20.

But what exactly did "redemption" mean? Certainly it meant overcoming national humiliation, democratic "party bickering," and physical suffering. But it meant more, otherwise the term, primarily a religious concept, would not have played such a role.

The virulence of the concept is certainly due to a tradition in Germany that goes back to the Napoleonic era in which national aspirations were expressed in the language of religious pathos. Between Napoleon's defeat of Prussia in 1806 and the beginning of the wars of liberation, i.e., during the period of Napoleon's greatest power and the German States' greatest weakness, Ernst Moritz Arndt published culture-critical essays and political pamphlets that called for German liberation. Arndt saw the struggle for freedom as an apocalyptic confrontation, a "final holy war" that would decide not only Germany's fate but that of the world. For Arndt, Napoleon was not a political opponent but the "ruler of darkness and enemy of the sons of light"; he was the "devil on the infernal throne" and, in short, "absolutely evil." According to Arndt, victory over Napoleon would not only make it possible to reestablish political order and social life but would inaugurate "the birth of a new age": "O rejoice! you have the promise of redemption."[14]

Out of the confrontation with Napoleon, Johann Gottlieb Fichte sketched a similar apocalyptic image: "If I understand God and His plan for the world correctly, and in all solemnity I believe I do, and if I have properly understood the figure that our enemy has presented throughout his public career (in which, of course, as a datum of history I could be wrong), so in him the full evil and enmity against God and freedom that the virtuous have opposed since the beginning of time have come together in a single instance armed with all the force evil can muster."[15] Fichte's stirring call did not use the word redemption but a Christian patriot could hardly fail to think of the Lord's Prayer and the words "deliver us from evil." In his *Addresses to the German Nation* Fichte contemplates the state of future national salvation: "It is

14 Ernst Moritz Arndt, *Geist der Zeit*, vols. 2 and 3, in *Sämtliche Werke*, vols. 9 and 10, ed. E. Schirmer (Magdeburg: Magdeburger Verlags – Anstalt, n.d.[1908]), vol. 9: 96, 128, 220; vol. 10, 110, 292, 299.

15 Johann Gottlieb Fichte, *Über den Begriff des wahrhaften Krieges in Bezug auf den Krieg im Jahre 1813 etc.* (Tübingen: In der Cottaischen Buchhandlung, 1815), Lecture III, 39.

in your hands [...] to become the starting point for the development of a new glorious age that will transcend all the ideas that you now have of one, so that from your generation posterity will date the year of its redemption."[16]

But apocalyptic hopes for redemption can be articulated under other political banners, too. Richard Wagner, for example, viewed the revolution of 1848 as "the redeemer of this vale of tears and the creator of a new world of happiness *for all*."[17] When the imminently expected revolution failed to take place he conceived of a future state of salvation in which the painful contradictions of human life would be sublimated into a world order both moral and aesthetic.[18] As Gottfried Benn noted, even before 1848 the idea of redemption had permeated *The Flying Dutchman* and *Tannhäuser*. Wagner and his wife Cosima later began to develop a new kind of religion that was to "make the human being into a real human being,"[19] i.e., one who would realize his own divinity and redeem himself. "You and I," he said to Cosima, "want to preach religion once again."[20] And in his last work, *Parsifal,* a "Bühnenweihfestspiel" (a Sacred Festival Play) that ends with the words "Highest holy Wonder! The Redeemer redeemed,"[21] he presents his religion in its aesthetic form. In this way, in his mind, he created the "artwork of the future" that granted him salvation "now" and at the same time made him the redeemer.[22]

16 Johann Gottlieb Fichte, "Reden an die deutsche Nation," in *Ausgewählte Werke in sechs Bänden*, ed. Fritz Medicus (Darmstadt: Wissenschaftliche Buchgesellschaft, 1962), vol. 5, 607.

17 Richard Wagner, "Die Revolution," in *Dichtungen und Schriften: Jubiläumsausgabe in zehn Bänden*, ed Dieter Borchmeyer (Frankfurt a. M.: Insel, 1983, vol. 5), 237.

18 Cf. Martin Gregor-Dellin, *Richard Wagner. Sein Leben, sein Werk, sein Jahrhundert* (Munich: Goldmann, 1980), and Jürgen Kühnel, *Parsifal: Erlösung dem Erlöser. Von der Aufhebung des Christentums in das Kunstwerk RichardWagners*, ed. Richard Wagner Verband Siegen (Cologne: Richard Wagner Verband, 1982).

19 Cosima Wagner, *Die Tagebücher*, ed. Martin Gregor-Dellin and Dietrich Mack (Munich: Piper, 1982, 2nd ed.), vol. 3, 556.

20 Ibid., 390.

21 Richard Wagner, "Parsifal: Ein Bühnenweihfestspiel (1877)," in *Dichtungen und Schriften*, vol. 4, 331.

22 Cf. Gregor-Dellin, *Richard Wagner*, 778 ff.; Kühnel, *Parsifal*, 38 ff.; Peter Wapnewski, *Der traurige Gott: Richard Wagner in seinen Helden* (Munich: DTV,

To be saved and at the same time be the redeemer is a very attractive idea, especially to those who like Wagner no longer felt at home in the Christian faith, or to those who had lost faith entirely. In the folkish movement of the Wilhelmine Empire various forms of German, or Teutonic, faith movements emerged that cultivated such ideas. The notions of redemption hoped for by these various communities were not identical, but all longed for an inner-worldly redemption, and often also for self-redemption. In 1892 the influential publisher Eugen Diederichs, "a genius at selling the works of all anti-bourgeois new religious figures in search of meaning or of those who claimed to have found one,"[23] wrote: "Man redeems himself; that is the new religion."[24] And painter and poet Ludwig Fahrenkrog, founder of the neo-pagan Germanic Faith Community, proclaimed: "I bring you the Gospel of self-redemption."[25]

The First World War brought with it numerous ideas of salvation in nationalistic form. They were modeled on Fichte's and Arndt's apocalyptic interpretations of history during the German wars against Napoleon, and they developed and spread similar interpretations of the World War. Fichte was never more popular than he was in 1914 and numerous new editions of his works appeared.[26] In speeches and sermons his name, next to Arndt's, was cited constantly. And consistent with the patterns of apocalyptic interpretation, Germany's enemies were decried as "beasts," "dragons," and

1978), 216; Hartmut Zelinsky, "Richard Wagners 'Kunstwerk der Zukunft' und seine Idee der Vernichtung," in *Von kommenden Zeiten. Geschichtsprophetien im 19. und 20. Jahrhundert*, eds. Joachim H. Knoll and Julius H. Schoeps (Stuttgart and Bonn, 1984), 84 ff.

23 Friedrich Wilhelm Graf, "Alter Geist und neuer Mensch. Religiöse Zukunftserwartungen um 1900," in *Das neue Jahrhundert: Europäische Zeitdiagnosen und Zukunftsentwürfe um 1900* ed. Ute Frevert (Göttingen: Vandenhoeck and Ruprecht 2000), 218.

24 Quoted in Justus H. Ulbricht, " '[...] in einer gottfremden, prophetenlosen Zeit [...].' Aspekte einer Problemgeschichte 'arteigener' Religion um 1900," in *Völkische Religion und Krisen der Moderne. Entwürfe 'arteigener' Glaubenssysteme seit der Jahrhundertwende,* eds. Stefanie v. Schnurbein, Justus H. Ulbricht (Würzburg: Königshausen and Neumann, 2001), 23.

25 Ibid, 27.

26 Cf. Hermann Lübbe, *Politische Philosophie in Deutschland* (Basel and Stuttgart: Schwabe, 1963), 201 seq.

"snakes," and all of them were viewed as incarnations of "the Antichrist." In countless war poems, sermons, and academic speeches one could read and hear that it was Germany's task to pass "final judgment" on its enemies. The authors of such texts expected an "ultimate victory," which "through suffering will free us from suffering." The nation's triumph would establish "a future Empire of Peace" in which Germany would "bring the sun to all peoples." With this view the hoped-for German victory took on the quality of an act of human self-redemption. Indeed, a pastor even coined the term "German redemption." As read in a war poem, the Germans were to be redeemed and at the same time be the redeemers:

> An image of men who redeem the world,
> Not because they chose themselves but because God chose them.[27]

After the war was lost, the longing for redemption was even greater, especially in folkish and nationalist circles. The hoped-for salvation was understood primarily in political terms as the "rebirth of the nation." But the Pan-German Max Robert Gerstenhauer who expressed these hopes in 1920 made it clear that the longed-for redemption also transcended politics. Gerstenhauer, who after the war was the National Grand Master of the Folkish German Federation, proclaimed a "spiritual and moral renewal and the rebirth of the German people" to be built on "Germanic religious reform."[28] This fusion of political, social, and religious hopes for redemption allows us to draw conclusions concerning the experiences of a spiritual need that awakened such longing. Naturally there was the defeat in 1918, the humiliating Treaty of Versailles, the unwanted and unloved Republic, and economic depression. But there were

27 All quotations: Klaus Vondung, "Geschichte als Weltgericht. Genesis und Degradation einer Symbolik," in *Kriegserlebnis. Der Erste Weltkrieg in der literarischen Gestaltung und symbolischen Deutung der Nationen,* ed. Klaus Vondung (Göttingen: Vandenhoeck and Ruprecht, 1980), 66 f.

28 Quoted in Uwe Puschner, *Die völkische Bewegung im wilhelminischen Kaiserreich. Sprache — Rasse — Religion* (Darmstadt: Wiss. Buchgesellschaft, 2001), 203; Uwe Puschner, "Weltanschauung und Religion – Religion und Weltanschauung. Ideologie und Form völkischer Religion," in *Zeitenblicke* 5 (2006), 1 (http://zeitenblicke.de/2006/1/Puschner/index.html; accessed: 06.22.2011).

also more deeply rooted feelings of deficiency and loss. Eugen Diederichs complained that he lived "in a godless age ruled by a cold reason that thought itself realistic" but which in fact "harbored an instinctive and inarticulate longing for religious renewal."[29] The Church's interpretation of the meaning of life had lost its appeal; this was particularly true of the Protestant churches from which neo-pagan religions recruited most of their followers. The "age of cold reason," i.e. of industrial society's rationalism and materialism, induced the longing for a new spiritual home. This desire for folk unity reveals that the differentiation and particularization of modern society was experienced as a deficit. One can describe the complex of motives that stood behind the often expressed yearning for redemption as a combination of national frustration, fundamental unease with modernity, and the feeling that life was devoid of meaning.

The desire for "redemption" was an intellectual phenomenon; it was intellectuals who formulated and propagated what Uwe Puschner has called "the doctrine of redemption."[30] In this regard Max Weber made a number of interesting observations: "The salvation sought by the intellectual is always based on inner need, and hence it is at once more remote from life, more theoretical, and more systematic than salvation from external distress, the quest for which is characteristic of non privileged strata. The intellectual seeks in various ways, the casuistry of which extends into infinity, to endow his life with a pervasive meaning, and thus to find unity with himself, with his fellow men, and with the cosmos. It is the intellectual who conceives of the 'world' as a problem of meaning."[31]

Of course, external distress is not reducible to mere material suffering and the national misery that followed the First World War. This distress, which so many intellectuals took to heart, can also develop into an "internal

29 Quoted in Ulbricht, *Völkische Religion und Krisen der Moderne*, 9: "[...] in einer gottfremden, prophetischen Zeit [...]."

30 Puschner, *Die völkische Bewegung im wilhelminischen_Kaiserreich*, 17. On the question of "religious intellectuals" cf. Graf, "Alter Geist und neuer Mensch," 199.

31 Max Weber, *Economy And Society: An Outline of Interpretative Sociology*, eds. Guenther Roth and Claus Wittich (Berkeley: University of California Press, 1978), 506.

distress." The intellectuals combined their search for personal meaning with the question of the meaning of the nation, and interpreted the latter as part of their own religious quest for redemption. Three examples from the 1920s illustrate how reactions to the plight of the nation merged with the search for personal meaning and the longing for redemption outside the lines of traditional Christian faith.

Rudolf Mirbt, a book seller and after the First World War a leader in the German Youth Movement (*Gaugraf des Wandervogels*)[32] in Stuttgart, in 1920 became the guide of a small group of young people, the *Jugendring* (Youth Circle) in Munich, which devoted itself primarily to amateur theater. As editor of the *Münchner Laienspiele* (Munich's Amateur Theater) and director of numerous amateur theater weeks in various parts of the country he became well-known and influential throughout the movement and was soon referred to as the "pope of amateur theater." In the autumn of 1923 he delivered a lecture on its principles to the Munich group. This was the year in which inflation peaked in Germany, French and Belgian troops occupied the Ruhr, in October communist uprisings took place in Hamburg, and on November 9th Hitler and Ludendorff staged a putsch in Munich. Mirbt began his lecture with the following words:

> *The young have discovered that we are no longer a people.* [...] Because we are not a people, we have no binding ties, neither to God nor man. [...] We live in an age that is church dominated, yet faithless and irreligious, an age that has forgotten how to pray, but we are no longer content to let ourselves be lulled to sleep by mysteries we don't understand. Rather we want to cry out to God. So let us have the courage to admit that perhaps it is the church and its liturgy that keeps us from Him.[33]

32 "Gaugraf des Wandervogels": Wandervogel (wandering bird) is the symbol and name of the German youth movement that began in Steglitz (Berlin) in 1896. "Graugraf" is the count who governs a shire.

33 Rudolf Mirbt, "Laienspiel," in idem, *Laienspiel und Laientheater. Vorträge und Aufsätze aus den Jahren 1923–1959* (Kassel: Bärenreiter, 1960), 9 and 15 (Emphasis in the original).

The role of amateur theater was to support the search for God. It favored "festival, celebration, and devotion."[34] Like Wagner's *Bühnenweihfestspiel*, although artistically more modest, it meant to provide redemption in aesthetic form. Amateur theater was to develop into the "great theater of the people" with the mission of creating a "people" again, i. e., a *Volksgemeinschaft* with a "religious mission."[35]

The writer Hanns Johst also looked for redemption, which he conceived as life in a re-born community endowed with aesthetic form and religious meaning. Johst began as an expressionist, writing primarily dramas that were not very successful. In the mid 1920s he drew close to National Socialism and in 1928 published *I Believe! Declarations of Faith*, a book in which he explained his new vision of redemption and the experiences that led to it. The year 1928 was a year of latent crisis. The period of economic growth had come to an end and the provisions of the Dawes Plan––and the fact that Germany still lacked full economic and financial sovereignty–– were felt as oppressive weights. In the Reichstag elections the German Social Democratic Party (SPD) and the German Communist Party (KPD) were the big winners, together gaining 42% of the mandates. As the year progressed signs of a new economic crisis could no longer be ignored and in winter the number of unemployed rose to more than two million.

Johst expected that a way out of the economic crisis would be found not through rational and practical action, but through the "rebirth of a community of faith." The "affliction, despair, and misery" of the people that Johst bewailed so volubly was an extrapolation of his own "inner need" from which he hoped to be redeemed: "We want to see that we have established a relationship to a new *Weltanschauung*, to the substance of the world's ideas. We want to be uplifted, we want to follow that part of the soul that liberates us and carries us to new heights and to an incomparable feeling of well-being."[36] It was obviously a profound experience of alienation that permitted such longings to grow so intense: "We all bear this fate in our soul, drawn into the raging vortex of an incomprehensible machinery, and

34 Ibid., 14.

35 Ignaz Gentges, Reinhard Leibrandt, Rudolf Mirbt, Bruno Sasowski, eds., *Das Laienspielbuch* (Berlin: Bühnenvolksbundverlag, 1929), 8.

36 Hanns Johst, *Ich glaube! Bekenntnisse* (Munich: Langen, 1928), 36, 74.

we therefore need this [liberating] experience as a confirmation of what we hoped for in vain in the uninterrupted and grueling day to day struggle for survival––namely, the sharp and sudden dissolution of all materialism, the logic of which threatens us with death."

As a writer Johst hoped that the new *Weltanschauung* would realize itself aesthetically in a cultic theater where he longed to experience the "dissolution of all materialism" and redemption from "inner need": "The more the day's distorted reality disappoints the hope of realizing this kind of ideal relief and redemption, the more naturally the soul in the theater at evening will experience itself as part of the community of those who share the same ideals, ethos, and faith, and who will thus be able to participate in the vision of truth."[37] Attempts during the Third Reich to establish such a cultic theater––in the form of outdoor theater (*Thingspiel*)––were unsuccessful and halted after just a few years. Johst was more successful in redeeming himself from the life of a struggling third rate writer. After 1933 he became a Prussian Councilor of State, President of the Reich Academy of Literature, President of the German Academy of Writers, Reich Senator for Culture, and SS Brigadier General.

By 1933 Joseph Goebbels had also received the recognition for which he had waited so long. On March 11, 1933, the Reich Ministry of Public Enlightenment and Propaganda was created for him and he wrote in his diary: "I'm elated. What a road it has been! Minister at thirty-five. Simply incredible."[38] If such a road to success brought back memories he would certainly have recalled the ups and downs along the way, periods of depression mixed with moments of euphoric hope. Nine years before he was appointed minister he had confided to his diary: "The road to redemption is long and over rich in sorrow, and we have to redeem ourselves or be redeemed."[39]

In October 1923 Goebbels started to keep a diary. At the time, he was a penniless young university graduate whose literary efforts were without success. He had returned to his parents' home in Rheydt and worked at the

37 Ibid., 75.

38 Elke Fröhlich, ed., *Die Tagebücher von Joseph Goebbels*, Part I, vol. 2/III (Munich: Saur, 2006), 145; (March 12, 1933).

39 Ibid., Part I, vol. 1/I, 137 (May 19, 1924).

occasional odd job. In 1924 he was drawn to National Socialism and soon became well known for his skill as an orator. In February of 1925 he was the managing director of the National Socialist Party section "West Germany" in Elberfeld. This was of course not a profession. His financial struggles continued and he had to turn repeatedly to his parents for help. In the NSDAP he wavered for awhile before deciding which leader to support. In the end he allied himself with Hitler, and indeed he more or less prostrated himself before him. In April 1926 he wrote: "I bow to the greater man, the political genius!" And a few days later and with typical emphasis he wrote: "Adolf Hitler, I love you!"[40] Hitler recognized Goebbels' talents as a propagandist and in November 1926 ordered him to Berlin as *Gauleiter* to lead the NSDAP there and direct its propaganda.

In his diaries between 1923 and 1926 Goebbels invoked the idea of redemption remarkably often. In contrast to the "religious intellectuals" discussed above who came from a Protestant milieu, Goebbels was Catholic. Perhaps this made it more difficult for him to take leave of his Christian faith. On New Year's Day, 1923, he wrote in his diary: "I know that Christ is my redeemer but I am not strong enough to follow in his footsteps and live a pure and selfless love."[41] Increasingly, Goebbels' desire was to "redeem myself"[42] which grew until it bordered on megalomania. He projected this personal longing into the leading figure of his novel *Michael*: "I am a hero, a god, a redeemer." "I am no longer a mere human being. I am a titan. A god!" "I have redeemed myself."[43] But ultimately Goebbels acknowledged that when it came to redeemers Adolf Hitler was his superior. On New Year's Day, 1926, he wrote in his diary: "At last, one man has become my leader and guide: Adolf Hitler. I believe in him."[44]

40 Ibid., Part I, vol. 1/II, Munich 2005, 73 (April 13, 1926); 76, (April 19, 1926).

41 Ibid., Part I, vol. 1/I, 67 (December, 31 1923).

42 Ibid., 136 (May 16, 1924).

43 Joseph Goebbels, *Michael. Ein deutsches Schicksal in Tagebuchblättern* [*Michael: Diary of a German Fate*] (Munich: Eher, 13th ed., 1938), 116, 127, 147. The novel was written between 1919 and 1923 with the title of *Michael Voormann*, but it was not until 1929, expanded and in part rewritten, that Goebbels was able to publish it in the party's own publishing house, Franz Eher.

44 Fröhlich, *Die Tagebücher von Joseph Goebbels*, Part I, vol. 1/I, 166 (December 31, 1926).

Goebbels' longing for salvation corresponded to experiences of need, imperfection, loss, and personal failure, which often plunged him into depression. He was not born into society's privileged classes and he therefore also suffered the external need of not having enough money,[45] at least until he went to Berlin. And of course his nationalist feelings suffered under the humiliations of his hometown Rheydt, which came under the occupation of the Rhineland by France and Belgium. All the external experiences of inadequacy, including his lack of success in getting started in a profession, the initial lack of recognition in the NSDAP, and the intrigues set against him by party comrades, combined to produce the feeling: "[I] live in a world of hate, greed, and slander."[46] These experiences merged with the feeling of his own inadequacy: "Thinking about oneself leads to despair." "Everyone is a rat, including me."[47] Even his sexual desire was a part of his existential despair. His lover, half-Jewish, as loving as she was could not help him: "In you I seek my redemption. In you? You can only give me a part of it."[48]

I believe that the above examples illustrate the history of the concept of redemption from the German wars against Napoleon to National Socialism and prepare the way for the study of its characteristics in detail. But it is important to remember that in all these instances we are dealing with the question of redemption in this world. The religious associations called forth by the term "redemption"—deliverance from evil, sin, and from the world as a vale of tears—were brought into play deliberately. The concept of redemption was always evoked with the intention of elevating issues into the religious sphere that otherwise might have been viewed pragmatically and seen simply for what they were, *responses* to the political, social, and material problems of practical life.

The main focus of the longed for redemption was the nation. From the time of Ernst Moritz Arndt until the 1920s, deliverance from national humiliation was a persistent theme. It was to liberate the people from the consequences of social differentiation and particularization. And the magic

45 Ibid., 249, 266, 288, 292, 307, 311, etc.

46 Ibid., 62 (December 31, 1923).

47 Ibid., Part I, vol. 1/II, 41 (January 4, 1926); 95, (June 12, 1926).

48 Ibid., Part I, vol. 1/I, 212 (August 25, 1924).

word for the hoped-for social redemption was *Volksgemeinschaft*, the community of the people that would supposedly be characterized by "unity" and "purity." Thus redemption was used as a battle cry in a cultural war against what was considered to be alien, provocative, and multiform—in short, "mixed" and therefore divisive and impure. For example, in 1934 Eugene Hadamovsky, appointed by Goebbels as Director of the Reich Radio, propagated the restructuring of the German radio service and personnel in terms of "redemption from social misfits, aesthetes, and alien elements (*Volksfremde*)."[49] The notion of deliverance from alien elements culminated in the desire for "deliverance from the Jews." Finally, for the individual the notion of existential redemption also included the hope of being freed from personal weaknesses and imperfections, of becoming important, of gaining recognition, and of finding fulfillment in love.

The tradition of emotionally charging politics with religion and the concept of redemption provided the basis of the Third Reich's use of the other forms of religiosity that we will explore in this book. Political faith became more important than membership in a party and political conviction and declarations of faith were celebrated in ritual events. The attempt to lend scientific or scholarly legitimacy to the meanings produced by this ideology took on the character of theology. Thus the justification of violently delivering the nation from the Jews was carried out in accordance with the thought-form of religious apocalypse. In various ways the paths to redemption offered by National Socialism appeared plausible to some. This occurred not in the way Daniel Goldhagen has argued, i.e., due to a quasi genetic German predisposition, but as the result of a mental and, indeed, habitual inclination that had been taught in the humanities and social sciences.

49 Eugen Hadamovsky, *Der Rundfunk im Dienste der Volksführung* (Leipzig: Noske, 1934), 11.

I had thought that I would be attending a mass demonstration and a political rally. But they celebrate a cult! And they conduct a liturgy; the great sacred ceremony of a religion.

Denis de Rougemont, *Journal d'Allemagne 1935–1936*

CHAPTER 1

POLITICAL RELIGION?

In *Mein Kampf* Hitler emphasized that the task of the National Socialist movement was "not a religious reformation, but the political reorganization of our people."[1] Without a doubt this statement expressed his real intention, and of course National Socialism was certainly a political movement with political goals. But at the same time National Socialism had religious aspects. Hitler helped to create them, especially with a vocabulary in which concepts like "faith" and "declaration of faith (confession)" played a central role. And, at least in part, he helped create the ritual of Party celebrations that recalled church ceremonies. He also let himself be hailed as the nation's "redeemer" and "messiah". And, finally, although he was probably unaware of it, the *Weltanschauung* and understanding of history that he propagated in *Mein Kampf* was based on a religious tradition of interpretation that is rooted in apocalyptic thought.

The religious character of National Socialism was noted by contemporary supporters as well as by critics. On May 14, 1933, in a letter to the *Kölnische Zeitung* (a Cologne newspaper) Romain Rolland arraigned "the brutality of the Brown Shirts," the "violent provocations," "racist pronouncements," and the "*auto-da-fés* of thought" that had taken place in the first months of National Socialist rule, and which were plain for everyone to see.[2] Thereupon, the *Kölnische Zeitung* mobilized a group of writers to reply to Romain Rolland with "declarations of faith in the new Germany." Among these was Rudolf G. Bindung (1867–1938), a conservative who had served at the front in the First World War and who at first supported National Socialism but later came to oppose its culture policy. In his reply to Rolland, he wrote: "An attempt on the part of the world to understand the nature of this revolution cannot emphasize too strongly the depth of its

1 Adolf Hitler, *Mein Kampf* (Munich: Eher, 349th-351st ed.,1938), 379.

2 Rudolf G. Bindung, et. al., *Sechs Bekenntnisse zum neuen Deutschland. Rudolf G. Bindung, E. G. Kolbenheyer, Die "Kölnische Zeitung", Wilhelm von Scholz, Otto Wirz, Robert Fabre-Luce antworten Romain Rolland* (Hamburg: Hanseatische Verlagsanstalt, 1933), 8–9.

religious roots: in its parades and symbols, in its flags and vows of loyalty, in its martyrs and fanatics, great and small, right down to the children, in its pronouncements and prophesies, in its implacable faith, and in the people's deep earnestness."[3] Here we see that it was primarily NS rituals that conveyed the impression of religiousness. Even Goebbels, who could be as cynical as he was enthusiastic, had the same reaction to the 1937 Nuremberg Party Congress and wrote in his diary: "A grand roll call of the SS and SA; a celebration that approaches the religious with ritual elements embedded in a fixed and unchanging tradition."[4]

Critics of National Socialism observed the same thing and drew the same conclusion, though of course like Denis de Rougemont interpreted them in a different light. As a young man this cultural philosopher from French-speaking West Switzerland spent 1935 and 1936 as a lecturer at the University of Frankfurt am Main. He carefully observed and chronicled everyday life in National Socialist Germany and two years later published his notes under the title *Journal d'Allemagne* . After attending a mass meeting of the NSDAP he stated that what he had seen had not been a "political rally" but "the great sacred ceremony of a religion."[5] De Rougemont concluded that the National Socialists were trying to do what the Jacobins had done during the French Revolution: "Here, as there, it is the attempt to found a purely national civic religion."[6] In his "Conclusion 1938" that he added to his published diary he states, "there is one point that certain events have made even more clear to me now, and which I cannot emphasize too strongly, namely the religious nature of Hitlerism."[7] He accused many other critics of National Socialism of not recognizing what was new and particular to its system of rule, namely that it was a "new totalitarian religion."[8] "The Saarland miners did not vote to join the Third Reich because they wanted

3 Ibid., 20.

4 Elke Fröhlich, *Die Tagebücher von Joseph Goebbels*. Part I, vol. 4 (Munich: Saur, 2000), 309.

5 Denis de Rougemont, *Journal d'Allemagne* (Paris 1938). Quoted and translated from the German edition: *Journal aus Deutschland 1935–1936* (Berlin: Aufbau, 2001), 60.

6 Ibid., 68 f.

7 Ibid., 87.

8 Ibid., 103.

to defend capitalism. Nor can one understand the fundamental phenomenon of re-creating a community on the basis of a feeling of the 'holy' by branding it 'hysterical.' Nor was it the desire for a political and legal tyranny that drove Austria into the arms of the *Fuehrer*, but the power of a religion, however primitive, to enthuse and win over the masses whose sense of belonging had been destroyed by a century of individualism."[9]

Denis de Rougemont was of course not the only person who grasped the novel and at the same time totalitarian nature of National Socialist religion. During the twenties and thirties a number of scholars and journalists used the term "secular religion" or "political religion" to describe totalitarian regimes––originally for Italian Fascism and Soviet Communism, and later for National Socialism.[10] In turn, the concept "totalitarian" was a neologism introduced into English by Luigi Sturzo, an Italian priest, Christian Democratic politician, and staunch opponent of Mussolini and Fascism. He immigrated to the United Kingdom in 1924 where he developed the concept and made it known through his publications. As early as 1926 he transferred the term from Italian Fascism to Bolshevism. Subsequently the concept spread, primarily through two books published in 1934 by the journalist and former editor in chief of *The London Times*, Wickham Steed, who applied the concept to National Socialism and made it into a general term for comparing dictatorships. Thus totalitarianism came to denote primarily a regime that wanted to control the human being's entire life, and not, as it once had, to refer simply to dictatorship as a form of State organization. This definition makes totalitarianism the antonym of the democratic and liberal understanding of politics and also of the Christian understanding of man. The insight that the totalitarian regime intervenes in the individual's sphere of spiritual self-understanding––and in this way violates the

9 Ibid., 90.

10 On the history of the concept, see Markus Huttner, *Totalitarismus und säkulare Religionen. Zur Frühgeschichte totalitarismuskritischer Begriffs- und Theoriebildung in Großbritannien* (Bonn: Bouvier, 1999); Emilio Gentile, *Le religioni della politica: Fra democrazie e totalitarismi* (Rome and Bari: Laterza, 2001); For the English translation, see *Politics as Religion* (Princeton and Oxford: University of Princeton Press, 2006), esp. 1–4; Emilio Gentile, "Political Religion: A Concept and its Critics: A Critical Survey," in *Totalitarian Movements and Political Religions*, 6:1 (2005), esp. 25–28.

border line between religion and the secular sphere—–is the basis for interpreting the totalitarian regime as a form of "secular religion."

In the thirties and during the Second World War those who adopted the interpretation of totalitarianism, such as Fritz Morstein Marx, Hans Kohn, Franz Borkenau, Sigmund Neumann, Raymond Aron and others, used the concept of secular religion in much the same way as the term "political religion" was used. The Italian historian Emilio Gentile has shown that the concept of political religion was not just an instrument of scientific analysis, but was used by the enemies of totalitarianism "to define a new phenomenon which was new and threatening, and for which the terms of traditional political language, such as, for instance, ideology, dictatorship, tyranny, despotism, appeared inadequate."[11]

Eric Voegelin occupies a special place among the authors who used the new interpretative concepts of secular religion and political religion. In 1938, a month after Hitler's invasion of Austria, his book *The Political Religions* was published by Bermann–Fischer in Vienna in its series *Ausblicke*. However, due to the new political situation only a few copies could be distributed. Voegelin, who had been an associate professor of political science and sociology at the University of Vienna, was stripped of his *venia legendi* in April 1938[12] and forced to emigrate, barely escaping the Gestapo.[13] In 1939, *The Political Religions* was reissued by Bermann–Fischer in Stockholm. In this work Voegelin provides a principle and theoretically based interpretation of National Socialism as a political religion.[14]

11 Gentile, *Political Religion: A Concept and its Critics*, 26.

12 Facsimile of the letter officially dismissing Voegelin from the faculty of Law and Political Science (*Rechts- und staatswissenschaftlichen Fakultät*) of the University of Vienna on April 23, 1938, in Jürgen Gebhardt ed., *Selected Correspondence 1924–1949. The Collected Works of Eric Voegelin*, vol. 29 (Columbia and London: University of Missouri Press, 2009), facing page 1.

13 Eric Voegelin, *Autobiographical Reflections* ed. Ellis Sandoz (Baton Rouge and London: LSU Press, 1964), 43, 54. Reprinted *in The Collected Works of Eric Voegelin. Vol. 34, Autobiographical Reflections. Revised Edition with a Voegelin Glossary and Cumulative Index*, ed. Ellis Sandoz (Columbia and London: University of Missouri Press, 2006).

14 For the place of this study in Voegelin's intellectual biography, his dismissal from the University of Vienna, and his emigration to the United States, see also Gebhardt ed., *Selected Correspondence 1924–1949*,"Editor's Introduction," 34–41.

Like de Rougemont, Voegelin also had to deal with the resistance that interpreting a political movement as religion calls forth. He attributed such resistance to the state of the language symbols that emerged following the institutional polarization of Church and State, which took place in the wake of the dissolution of the western Christian Empire and ushered in the modern world of national States. "The concepts of religion and politics followed the institutions and their symbols: they entered onto the battlefield and placed themselves under the authority of the linguistic symbols used in the struggle. For this reason, cognition today still involves the contrasts formed under the pressure of their conceptual instruments, although a critical look might reveal merely different examples of the effectiveness of closely related fundamental human forces."[15]

Voegelin found these fundamental forces in the deep stirrings of the soul that are occasioned by the experience of creatureliness. According to Voegelin, from this experience arises the longing to transcend the limits of human existence and to find redemption through participation in a world-transcending and all-encompassing whole. "The Beyond surrounding us can be searched for and found in all the directions in which human existence is open toward the world: in the body and in the spirit, in man and in community, in nature (*Natur*) and in God."[16] Voegelin calls the seeking and finding in which the "agitations of existence" take place and are fulfilled the "spiritual-religious experience": "Wherever a reality discloses itself in the religious experience as sacred, it becomes the most real, a *realissimum*. This basic transformation from the natural to the divine results in a sacral and value-oriented recrystallization of reality around that aspect that has been recognized as being divine. Worlds of symbols, linguistic signs and concepts arrange themselves around the sacred center; they firm up as systems, become filled with the spirit of religious agitation and fanatically defended as the 'right' order of being."[17]

15 Erich Voegelin, *Die politischen Religionen* (Vienna: Bermann – Fischer, 1938), 8–9. Quoted from Eric Voegelin, *The Political Religions*, in *The Collected Works of Eric Voegelin*, vol. 5, 27.

16 Voegelin, *Die Politischen Religionen*,14f. Quoted from *The Collected Works of Eric Voegelin*, vol. 5, 31.

17 Ibid., 15f. Quoted from *The Collected Works of Eric Voegelin*, vol. 5, 31–32.

Thus Voegelin did not interpret National Socialism as a political religion just because it used a religious vocabulary and developed cultic forms of celebration, but because his analysis revealed the religious nature of its existential core. Voegelin's studies showed that the religious needs of a secularized world can be diverted to partial contents of the world which, having manifested themselves as sacred, become objects of faith. In the case of National Socialism this partial content was "race," which was elevated to the status of the meaning-giving center of order: Voegelin calls the "community of the people" (*Volksgemeinschaft*) that is legitimated by being elevated to sacred status, a "particular ecclesia" and contrasts it to Christianity's "universal ecclesia."[18]

With few exceptions,[19] in the immediate aftermath of the Second World War Voegelin's analysis of political religions and his heuristic concepts were not taken up by historians in their analysis of National Socialism. By contrast, the concept of totalitarianism experienced a renaissance in the fifties and sixties through the pioneering studies of Hannah Arendt, Carl Joachim Friedrich, and Zbigniew Brzezinski.[20] However, in the seventies it was no longer in the foreground of the public debate. Marxist oriented scholars and leftist intellectuals rejected it on principle because it not only compared fascism and communism but viewed them as equivalents.

Following the collapse of the communist regimes in Central and Eastern Europe after 1989, a new interest grew in comparing 20th century dictatorships. In view of the novelty and level of political violence in which the Soviet Union, Fascist Italy, and National Socialist Germany had engaged, the question arose of whether––despite obvious differences––they

18 Ibid., 33, 54–56. Cf. *The Collected Works of Eric Voegelin*, vol. 5, 44–47, 64–66.

19 Hans-Jochen Gamm, *Der braune Kult. Das Dritte Reich und seine Ersatzreligion. Ein Beitrag zur politischen Bildung* (Hamburg: Rütten and Loenin, 1962); Friedrich Heer, *Der Glaube des Adolf Hitler. Anatomie einer politischen Religiosität* (Munich and Eßlingen: Bechtle, 1968); Klaus Vondung, *Magie und Manipulation. Ideologischer Kult und politische Religion des Nationalsozialismus* (Göttingen: Vandenhoeck and Ruprecht, 1971).

20 Hannah Arendt, *The Origins of Totalitarianism* (New York: Harcourt and Brace, 1951); Carl Joachim Friedrich and Zbigniew Brzezinski, *Totalitarian Dictatorship and Autocracy* (Cambridge, MA: Harvard University Press, 1956).

did not share common elements. In order to conceptualize these elements of modern violent regimes, the last twenty years have seen a reactivation of the terms "totalitarianism" and "political religion." Eric Voegelin's 1938 study was republished in 1993[21] and played a role in rekindling an interest in political religion as a heuristic concept. The political scientist Hans Maier, a Munich colleague of Voegelin before Voegelin returned to the United States following his retirement in 1969, directed a multi-year research project in the 1990s on "Totalitarianism and Political Religions" that produced a comprehensive three volume work.[22] Other scholars followed in the 1990s and studies have continued into the new century.[23] In 2000 the journal *Totalitarian Movements and Political Religions* was founded. Since that time a number of volumes have appeared that emphasize new aspects.[24] Recently Emilio Gentile in two books and in numerous articles has systematized and enriched the discussion of the concept of political religion.[25]

21 Eric Voegelin, *Die politischen Religionen* ed. Peter J. Opitz (Munich: Fink, 1993).

22 Hans Maier ed., *Totalitarismus und politische Religionen. Konzepte des Diktaturvergleichs*. vol. 1. (Paderborn: Schöningh, 1996); Hans Maier and Michael Schäfer, eds., *Totalitarismus und politische Religionen. Konzepte des Diktaturvergleichs*. vol. 2. (Paderborn: Schöningh, 1997); Hans Maier ed., *Totalitarismus und politische Religionen*. vol. 3: *Deutungsgeschichte und Theorie* (Paderborn: Schöningh, 2003).

23 Cf. Michael Ley and. Juius H. Schoeps, eds., *Der Nationalsozialismus als politische Religion* (Bodenheim: Philo-Verlag Gesellschaft, 1997); Claus-Ekkehard Bärsch, *Die politische Religion des Nationalsozialismus. Die religiösen Dimensionen der NS-Ideologie in den Schriften von Dietrich Eckart, Joseph Goebbels, Alfred Rosenberg und Adolf Hitler* (Munich: Fink, 1998, 2nd rev. ed., 2002); Michael Ley, Heinrich Neisser, and Gilbert Weiss, eds., *Politische Religion? Politik, Religion und Anthropologie im Werk von Eric Voegelin* (Munich: Fink, 2003); Roger Griffin, Robert Mallett and John Tortorice, eds., *The Sacred in Twentieth-Century Politics. Essays in Honour of Professor Stanley G. Payne* (New York: Palgrave and Macmillan, 2008).

24 Michael Burleigh, Emilio Gentile and Robert Mallett, eds., *Totalitarian Movements and Political Religions* (Milton Park, Abingdon: Taylor and Francis, 2000 seq.).

25 Emilio Gentile, *Il culto del littorio: La sacralizzatione della politica nell'Italia fascista* (Rome 2001); Emilio Gentile, *Le religioni della politica*; english title, *Politics as Religion*.

Nevertheless, the heuristic concept of political religion is still controversial. Many critics are reluctant to use the term "religion" for an anti-Christian (and above all anti-Jewish and anti-Semitic) ideology. Concerned that under this name National Socialism might appear to be just another variant of Christianity, although a perverted one, they propose the alternative of "*ersatz* religion" or "religion's *ersatz*" in order to express the derivative and instrumental character of the religion of National Socialism.[26] German historians who study National Socialism generally ignore the heuristic concept of political religion or reject it with the claim that it has no analytical value. Hans Mommsen is a representative of this view. Although he concedes that one can find "pseudo-religious elements in the cult of Hitler," he argues that "National Socialism lacked the ideological substance to do more than simulate a 'political religion'": "The decisive objection to applying the theory of political religion to National Socialism is that it attributes an ideological rigor and consistency to a movement that lacked any and which in every way was a mere imitative movement."[27]

Thus in Germany it is primarily in political science, sociology, and cultural studies that the concept of political religion has been used to interpret 20th century totalitarian regimes. On the other hand, outside Germany—and this is a notable difference—a number of renowned historians work with this heuristic concept.[28] One of them, Emilio Gentile, has convincingly systematized the concepts of political or secular religions and developed important criteria that demonstrate how some modern political movements became "religions." "Modern political movements are transformed into secular religions when they: (a) define the meaning of life and

26 See also, Hans Buchheim, "Despotie, Ersatzreligion, Religionsersatz," in *Totalitarismus und politische Religionen*, ed. Maier, vol. 1, 260–263.

27 Hans Mommsen, "Nationalsozialismus als politische Religion," in *Totalitarismus und politische Religionen*, eds. Maier and Schäfer, vol. 2, 179–181.

28 For example, Philippe Burrin, University of Geneva; Roger Griffin, Oxford Brookes University; Emilio Gentile, University La Sapienza in Rome; Marina Cattaruzza, University of Bern; Stanley G. Payne, University of Wisconsin in Madison; Michael Burleigh, originally at the University of Cardiff, since 2000 at Washington and Lee University in Lexington, Fellow of the Royal Historical Society and founder of the journal *Totalitarian Movements and Political Religions*.

ultimate ends of human existence; (b) formalise the commandments of a public ethic to which all members of these movement must adhere; and (c) give utter importance to a mythical and symbolic dramatisation in their interpretation of history and reality, thus creating their own 'sacred history,' embodied in the nation, the State or the party, and tied to the existence of a 'chosen people,' which is glorified as the regenerating force of all mankind."[29]

Voegelin demonstrated that by elevating a particular area of reality to the "most real," "a sacral and value-oriented recrystallization of reality" forms around that which has been recognized as divine. In this sense the political religion of National Socialism does indeed have a dogmatic center and a certain "rigor and consistency." At its core we find the concept of race, or blood. Around this holy center we find the *Volk* (people) as the substantial bearer of the blood. In further rings around this center we find the *Volksgemeinnschaft* as the sacralized unity of the people, the *Boden* (soil) that nourishes it, and the *Reich* (Empire) that articulates its will, and finally the *Fuehrer* as the representative of the people and the empire.

Yet despite a measure of dogmatic coherency, scepticism with regard to the concept of political religions is justified. As de Rougemont pointed out, compared to the tenets of traditional religions, the dogmas of National Socialism are not only primitive but "the horrible thing is they are also empty."[30] In other words, the main dogmas of the National Socialist religion—race and the Community of the People—have no place in reality. There is no such thing as "racially pure blood," and the unified *Volksgemeinschaft* is the projection of a dream. The only concrete reality is the *Fuehrer* himself, and the ritual elevation of the leader to a sacrosanct figure clearly serves the purpose of supporting his claim to unlimited power.

One justified objection to the use of the concept is that it suggests the political religion of National Socialism was a homogenous phenomenon, which it was not. Although we find at its core religiously charged racism and an apocalyptic world view in which most of the leading National Socialists believed, there were significant differences in the religious orientations of Hitler and Himmler, and of Goebbels and Rosenberg. There were

29 Gentile, "Political Religion: A Concept and its Critics," 29 .

30 De Rougemont, *Journal aus Deutschland*, 90, 118.

also differences between the organizers of the National Socialist "religion" and their faithful followers. And there were various forms of religious expression, from the centrally directed cultic mass celebrations all the way down to the various states of individual religious enthusiasm.

In this connection it is worth remembering that in his later work Eric Voegelin did not use the concept of political religions, although his 1938 study provided fruitful impulses for further research. In his dictated *Autobiographical Reflections* (1973) he noted: "When I spoke of the *politischen Religionen* I conformed to the usage of a literature that interpreted ideological movements as a variety of religion. [...] The interpretation is not all wrong, but I would no longer use the term *religions* because it is too vague." He no longer found it justifiable to subsume the historical and substantial differences between such diverse phenomena as the spiritual movement of Akhenaton, theories from the Middle Ages, and Thomas Hobbes' *Leviathan* under the concept of political religions, and to bring these together with National Socialism. According to Voegelin an adequate treatment of the problem would have to take into account the "far-reaching differentiations."[31]

Thus we must raise the question of how we should proceed with the concept of political religion? First, I do not think that we have to be too cautious in our use of it. That seems unnecessary if we confine ourselves to using the term in the sense of a concept of religious phenomenology, as Emile Durkheim recommended. In this regard one recognizes a religion by the fact that its followers hold a particular creed which they express and practice in rituals.[32] National Socialism as a political religion fulfills the criteria of this minimal definition. The analysis of its concrete forms of expression calls for the kind of cautious use of the term recommended by Stanley G. Payne: "The concept of PR has proven useful not as an absolute definition of a *ding an sich* (Thing-in-itself) but simply as a heuristic device for the analysis of strong ideology and its cultic practices. It helps to explain the character and function of the major new ideologies in a largely secular era."[33] In order to fulfil the

31 Voegelin, *Autobiographical Reflections*, 50–51.

32 Emile Durkheim, *Die elementaren Formen des religiösen Lebens* (Frankfurt: Suhrkamp 3rd ed., 1984), 22, 61, 67, 75.

33 Stanley G. Payne, "On the Heuristic Value of the Concept of Political Religion and its Application," in *The Sacred in Twentieth-Century Politics*, 33.

requirements of a differentiated view of the phenomena that are to be studied, Emilio Gentile's definition of political, or secular, religion is of great value.

When in what follows I occasionally use the term "political religion" it is in the sense discussed above and with the mentioned reservations. The concept of political religion is not the leading category in this book. And I have chosen another approach to the phenomena precisely because there is no homogenous political religion in National Socialism. In what follows I will present and analyze the various forms in which religiosity is articulated in National Socialism, giving each of the fundamental religious phenomena a separate chapter.

"Faith" played a central role in National Socialist discourse, from Hitler and his paladins down to enthusiastic young writers like Herbert Böhme and Gerhard Schumann. Appeals to faith and confessions of faith served various purposes, and their several functions will be elucidated. Indeed in National Socialism *mystical* fanaticism could be joined to racism; Alfred Rosenberg provides the prime example of this type of thought. According to Gentile, when modern political movements are transformed into secular religions, history and reality are interpreted as a mythical drama and turned into the sacred history of a nation or a party. This is precisely what took place in National Socialism. The *myth* into which the history of the National Socialist movement was transformed was further consecrated by being constantly renewed in ritual celebrations. However *ritual* was just one part of the all encompassing *cult* that was developed in the Third Reich, and which was intended to define public and private life politically, culturally, and religiously. The Third Reich's most impressive ritual celebrations took place in mass meetings, to whose effects many intellectuals also succumbed. However the intellectuals wanted to express their faith and conviction in more sophisticated ways than the average person, and they engaged in a discourse whose structure and vocabulary amounted to a kind of theology. Ultimately the murderous effects of the National Socialist regime of violence were the result of an interpretation of the world and history that Hitler shared with many of his followers and which is of religious origin: The *Apocalypse*.

German youth! Above denomination and class declare your faith in the eternal truth of our God-sent *Fuehrer* and his sacred flag!

Reich Youth Leader Baldur von Schirach on the occasion of the 1935 summer solstice celebration.

CHAPTER 2

FAITH

Denis de Rougemont was so impressed by Hitler's statement quoted in the newspapers that he referred to it twice in his diary: "I can only live if my deep faith in the German people is strengthened again and again by the German people's trust and faith in me!"[1] De Rougemont was impressed and at first irritated because in Hitler's speech religious language played an important role in what was palpably a political context. Indeed, in the context of faith what normally would have been termed "political persuasion" and "political following" was raised to the level of religion, just as the concept of redemption was elevated to the sphere of religion. A pragmatic understanding of politics would have simply referred to this as *responses* to political and other practical problems. In De Rougemont's view, Hitler's insistence on "faith" established a relationship of competition with the churches and with the Christian faith.

Without a doubt this "faith" had religious roots. In *Mein Kampf* Hitler stated that the model for his political activity was religious faith. On the importance of faith he wrote: "Without a clearly defined faith, religiousness in its many and vague forms would not only be worthless for human life, but probably contribute to its dissolution."[2] Hitler went so far as to refer to the Catholic Church as his model: "Here again we can learn from the Catholic Church. [...] It has seen clearly that its powers of resistance do not lie in adapting doctrine more or less to the latest findings of science, since, in reality, these are always changing, rather its strength lies in holding fast to established dogma; this alone endows the whole with the character of faith."[3] Hitler drew conclusions for his political struggle in accord with this observation: "From general ideas, a political program has to be drawn up, and from a general *Weltanschauung* a political faith must be formed."[4] The role Hitler

1 Denis de Rougemont, *Journal aus Deutschland 1935–1936* (Berlin: Aufbau, 2001).

2 Adolf Hitler, *Mein Kampf* (Munich: Eher, 349th-351st ed., 1938), 417.

3 Ibid., 512 f.

4 Ibid., 418.

saw for himself was pretty clear: "One man must arise and with apodictic conviction bring granite principles into the otherwise vacillating world of notions held by the broad masses and then fight for the exclusive right of these principles for as long as it takes, until out of the mind's fluctuating thought arises the rock that unites the wills of the many into one faith."[5]

As theology, religious studies, and the sociology of religion show, in every religion faith is the attitude "that one takes toward divinity,"[6] or toward what one has experienced to be and recognizes as "holy." In addition, faith can be defined as "one of the possible paths to redemption."[7] Naturally, faith can only be determined in relation to its object.[8] For only then does the nature of a particular faith come concretely into view along with its differences with expressions of faith in other religions.

As far as the faith of National Socialists is concerned its articles are well known: Blood and Soil, *Volk* and *Reich*, and naturally the *Fuehrer* and the flag which symbolizes faith's objects as the cross symbolizes Christian faith. Even National Socialism and its political organization––in other words, the political religion and its "church"––could be raised to objects of faith; for example, by a political leader in his address to a harvest celebration: "I believe in National Socialism and in the Party as the bearer of its idea!"[9] Indeed the National Socialist articles of faith took on the character of religious dogma. In Hitler's view what he had written in *Mein Kampf* on the importance and function of religious dogma was obviously also true for the State as he understood it: "If religious doctrine and faith are really to reach the broad masses, then only through the unconditional authority of its content; this is the exclusive foundation of any faith's effectiveness. [...] Therefore, the attack on dogma as such, is always a fight against the general legal foundations of the State."[10] After

5 Ibid., 419 (Emphasis in the original).
6 Article entitled "Glaube" in *RGG*, 3rd ed., vol. 3, col. 1586; Cf. the article "Glaube" in *RGG*, 4th ed., vol. 4; *LThK*, 3rd ed., vol. 4: *HWPh*, vol. 3; Emile Durkheim, *Die elementaren Formen des religiösen Lebens*. 3rd ed. (Frankfurt: Suhrkamp, 1984), 22–75.
7 *RGG*, 3rd ed., vol. 3, col. 1586.
8 Ibid., col. 1587; Durkheim, *Die elementaren Formen des religiösen Lebens*, 67–70.
9 *Vorschläge*, 10004.
10 Hitler, *Mein Kampf*, 293.

Hitler took power in 1933 the National Socialist articles of faith were to have absolute validity. In his closing speech at the 1934 Party Congress in Nuremberg Hitler announced his intention of demanding a declaration of faith from all Germans: "More will be expected 'of members of the Party' than from the millions of other National Comrades (*Volksgenossen*). For the former it is not enough to confess, 'I believe' [which was obviously to be required of the 'millions of other *Volksgenossen*'], but the oath, 'I fight!'"[11]

The act of professing faith is a much stronger commitment than the willingness to declare that one will adhere to a party program—it is a "sacred" commitment. The National Socialist regime's most important way of promoting the propagation of faith and bringing about declarations of faith was its celebrations: from the roll call at the Reich Party Congress with its consecration of flags, to the swearing-in ceremonies for new members of the Party or the SS, to the morning roll call of the Hitler Youth at vacation camps. The functions of recalling the National Socialist articles of faith and of supporting them with liturgical forms of declarations of faith were realized in an exemplary manner in choral literature, for example in *The Commitment* (*Die Verpflichtung*) by Eberhard Wolfgang Möller. This choral poetry was used for the celebrations of initiation into the *Jungvolk* (ages 10–14) and the Hitler Youth[12] (ages 14–18), the Party organizations for children and adolescents, as well as in other Party structures. It was first performed in the Marienburg[13] on January 24, 1935, in a ceremony consecrating *Jungvolk* flags at the supra-regional organizational level (*Jungbann*). This was the anniversary of the death of Herbert Norkus, a member of the Hitler-Youth and a martyr and model for the HJ, as Horst Wessel was for the SA. The ceremony was broadcast over all Reich radio stations and could be, and usually was, integrated into local HJ initiation ceremonies as a "community-radio-reception" (*Gemeinschaftsempfang*). The liturgical text lets heralds demand that the truths of faith be proclaimed in a revelatory "vision":

11 *Der Kongreß zu Nürnberg vom 5. bis 10. September 1954. Offizieller Bericht über den Verlauf des Reichsparteitages mit sämtlichen Reden* (Munich: Eher,1935), 211.

12 Hereafter referred to as HJ.

13 A castle of the Teutonic Order in East Prussia, today Poland.

> Speak, what you have seen, and proclaim what you believe,
> That we may confess what we long to believe.[14]

Three "proclamations" follow and at the end of each all confess the central dogmas of the National Socialist faith:

> We believe in the blood [...].
> We believe in the soil[...].
> We believe in the people [...].[15]

Other liturgical texts consecrate Hitler as a holy person, sometimes with the use of Christian symbols: "And know that we need him / like bread and wine."[16] The *Fuehrer* is given the god-like status of the redeemer who is the answer incarnate to the community's and the individual's existential questions. Even in the descriptive language of scholars of constitutional law (*Staatsrecht*) this god-like position is presented as super-human and omnipotent. In 1934 the constitutional law expert Ernst Rudolf Huber, who next to Ernst Forsthoff was Carl Schmitt's most important student, explained: "The *Fuehrer* and the movement that is bound to him by sacred bonds (*Gefolgschaft*) acts out of the totality of the idea of the people and the reality of the people. [...] The *Fuehrer* is at one with the idea, it acts through him. But he is also the idea, the one who is able to endow the idea with living form. [...] *He represents the people*, not in the sense of looking out for their interests like a business director, or acting in accordance with the terms of a contract, but in the real sense that he visibly embodies and symbolizes the unity of the people. [...] The *Fuehrer's* rule is absolute and requires no external limitation because it is its own measure."[17]

14 Eberhard Wolfgang Möller, *Die Verpflichtung* (Berlin: Langen Müller, 1935), 7.

15 Ibid., 8, 10, 13.

16 Gerhard Schumann, *Gedichte und Kantaten* (Munich: Langen/Müller, 1940), 44.

17 Ernst Rudolf Huber, "Die Totalität des völkischen Staates," in *Die Tat. Monatsschrift für die Zukunft deutscher Kultur* 26, 1 (1934), 37 f (Italics in the original spaced).

With the *Fuehrer* as the incarnation of the sacred national community he is also the object of declarations of faith. The preferred text for this was the "German Prayer" written by Herbert Böhme:

Under these flags let us declare:
We are Germans.
We follow our Fuehrer
As the command incarnate
Of a higher law
That lives above us and in us,
Which we divine,
And in which we believe.
We believe in our Fuehrer
As a revelation
Of this law
For us,
His people.[18]

In the Third Reich the National Socialist celebrations were intended primarily as "declarations (or confessions) of faith" designed to bring the participants into a "community of faith" (*Bekenntnisgemeinde*); this was underlined repeatedly in the suggestions and guidelines for organizing celebrations.[19] The Party's publications made it unmistakably clear why this was so important. Such celebrations were not merely expressions of an ideological or political commitment but were intended to bring about "confessions of faith" that embrace *the entire human being*. In this sense a 1942 article on principles in *Die neue Gemeinschaft* (The New Community) conjured up the image of "the inexorable penetration of all spheres of life's expression with the Movement's idea, and in this way of winning the whole German human being for the totality, unity, and exclusivity of our

18 Herbert Böhme, *Das deutsche Gebet* (Munich: Eher, 1936), 7.
19 E.g. *Vorschläge*, April 1935, 3: Karl Seibold, "Die Grundsätze der Feiergestaltung im Schulungslager," in *Fest- und Freizeitgestaltung im NSLB*, vol. 1 (1936/3), 10; This is repeated in a similar manner in other directory journals, see esp. *DnG*.

Weltanschauung."[20] In the same year the journal expressed a further fundamental principle that described precisely the psycho-social function of celebrations as "confessions of faith" and indicated the political goals that were to be pursued. The celebrations should be "a regularly recurring ceremonious appeal to the depths of the soul (*Seelenkraft*) of every individual member of the Party and people in order that, through regularly repeated declarations of commitment to the community, this firm and deep well of faith will flow over into the national community and, overcoming all apathy, will enable the nation to grow stronger and stronger." Appropriately enough this fundamental article closes with a *Fuehrer* quote: "He who has faith in his heart has the strongest force in the world!"[21] Even before the outbreak of war the publications concerned with Party celebrations emphasized that their purpose was to help "strengthen faith in the *Fuehrer* and the people" and thus to strengthen "the will to commitment and action,"[22] or that, and even more openly, from faith and the confession of faith comes the willingness to sacrifice.[23] During the war the sequence of faith, confession, and the willingness to sacrifice came into its own.

The Third Reich required confessions of faith but the authorities did not need to apply force to get them. Many Germans believed in the *Fuehrer* and the National Socialist dogmas. Of course, and excluding for a moment the dogmatic center of National Socialist faith, there were various degrees of intensity and differing shades of belief, as well as different motives for and attitudes toward it. This can be illustrated by a few examples.

In his diaries between 1923 and 1926, the young Joseph Goebbels often revealed the precarious state of his soul, his despair and longing for redemption, and his struggle to believe. On September 22nd, 1924, he wrote: "Am I on the right path? Sometimes I'm plagued by doubt. Oh, if I could only find an unshakeable and unerring faith!!!"[24] A few days later he put doubt

20 *DnG*, May 1942, nr. 5, 213.

21 *DnG*, Nov. 1942, nr.11, 595 f.

22 *Freude – Zucht – Glaube. Handbuch für die kulturelle Arbeit im Lager. Im Auftrage der Reichsjugendführung der NSDAP* ed. Claus Dörner (Potsdam: Ludwig Voggenreiter, 1937), 71.

23 Seibold, *Die Grundsätze der Feiergestaltung*, 8.

24 Elke Fröhlich, *Die Tagebücher von Joseph Goebbels*, Part I, vol. 1/I (Munich: Saur, 2004), 227.

aside and encouraged himself: "I seek the new Reich and the new human being! I will only find them in faith! Faith in the mission that is in us will lead to final victory! *Heil*!"[25] In 1926 his longing for faith found an end because in that year he decided to bow to the "the greater man, the political genius."[26] On New Year's Eve he wrote in his diary: "At last, one man has become my leader and guide: Adolf Hitler. I believe in him."[27] He remained firm in this faith and after Hitler's suicide on April 30th, 1945, succeeded him as Reich Chancellor for a few days before committing suicide himself.

Middle level National Socialist functionaries did not hesitate to declare their faith in National Socialist dogma and one can assume that they internalized it. Eugen Hadamovsky is a good example. Named National Program Director for German Radio, he was without a doubt one of the most capable men who put radio into the service of National Socialist propaganda. And his writings reveal that the organizational talent he invested in German radio was based on a mission of faith. His fundamental position was that the Third Reich "will not have the structure of a State but of a community of faith in the service of the missionary struggle for National Socialism." He understood the community's true articles of faith to be "the great laws of Blood and Soil and of *Volk* and Race,"[28] and viewed the radio service that he had reorganized as the "avant garde of faith."[29]A year after the regime came to power Hadamovsky wrote that because of all media, the newest "is the least weighed down by the traditions of a baleful past." National Socialist radio "in the hands of ardent and determined activists has advanced to be the professor and missionary of National Socialism": "It is the faithful bearer of the idea."[30]

In matters of faith, the young and fanatical supporters of National Socialism are particularly interesting. In *The Political Religions* Voegelin devoted a brief final chapter to "Belief" (*Glaube*), to the "movements of the

25 Ibid., 231 (27th September1924).

26 Ibid., Part I, vol. 1/II. (Munich 2005), 73 (13th April1926).

27 Ibid., 166 (31st December1926).

28 Eugen Hadamovsky, *Der Rundfunk im Dienste der Volksführung* (Leipzig: Noske,1934), 12 f.

29 Ibid., 19.

30 Eugen Hadamovsky, *Dein Rundfunk. Das Rundfunkbuch für alle Volksgenossen* (Munich: Eher, 1934), 69.

soul"[31] that shaped the religious inner life of National Socialist believers. His exemplary analysis was based on a small collection of poems by Gerhard Schumann, *Songs of the Reich*. Presumably the thin volume published in 1935 came into his hands by accident, but through Schumann he had come into contact with the believing National Socialist *par excellence*. Schumann may be regarded as representative of many National Socialists, especially for a group of writers born between 1905 and 1914, i.e., Hans Baumann, Herbert Böhme, Kurt Eggers, Herybert Menzel, Eberhard Wolfgang Möller, Hans Jürgen Nierentz, and Baldur von Schirach. Most were university educated although not all of them completed their studies. The decisive formative years as youths and young men, their student years, and the often hopeless pursuit of a profession took place between the world economic crisis and 1933. Most were unable to find a profession until after 1933, aided by the NSDAP or as functionaries in the Party itself. As writers they first published in the Third Reich. Characteristic of all of them is the fact that their literary works express faith in National Socialism.

Gerhard Schumann, the son of a school teacher, was born in 1911 and as a student in the Protestant theological seminaries of Schöntal and Urach experienced an intensive religious socialization. These experiences certainly shaped the attitude toward faith that he later developed in National Socialism and its *Fuehrer*. He was a talented lyrical poet but remained an epigone. In 1934 he interrupted the university studies he began in 1930 in order to add politics to his activity as a writer. In his political career he held numerous positions, some quite high, in the NSDAP, the SA, the Reich Propaganda Directorate, and the Reich Culture Senate. Following two years of military service during the war, and only thirty years old, he became the head dramaturge of the Württemburg State Theater in Stuttgart and later the theater's deputy director.

In his interpretation of the *Songs of the Reich,* Voegelin found that the poems' religious movements have their source in the "basic emotion of natural abandonment (*kreatürlichen Verlassenheit*)": "The basis of natural abandonment (*kreatürliche Verlassenheit*) is described as a state of dreamlike

31 Eric Voegelin, *The Political Religions*, in *The Collected Works of Eric Voegelin*, vol. 5, *Modernity without Restraint,* ed. Manfred Henningsen (Columbia/London: University of Missouri Press, 2000), 19–75. Here, 67.

unreality, of coldness, of sealed-off loneliness. The soul breaks out of this state with a burning fervor to be united with the sacred whole. A hot flood of excitement tears it from its solitude," and "lets the soul flow into the whole of the people. The soul becomes depersonalized in the course of finding and unification, it frees itself completely of the cold ring of its own self [...]. By losing its own self it ascends to the grander reality of the people."[32]

We are already familiar with these "movements of the soul" through our acquaintance with Hanns Johst's book, significantly entitled *I Believe!*, which expresses the experience of "creaturely abandonment" as "want," "despair," "restlessness," "torture," "loneliness," and feeling the "helplessness of a child." Johst hoped to find "relief and redemption" in the "community of those with the same ethos, the same will, and the same faith" into which the individual would merge and where the restless search for redemption would finally know peace in a "new and incomparable feeling of well-being."[33] In the case of Schumann, when we consult other works besides the *Songs of the Reich* we encounter further aspects of the soul's movements that build the basis of faith in National Socialism.

The experience of creaturely abandonment and of creatureliness *per se* finds its sharpest form in death. Death is therefore the strongest impulse for the search for redemption and at the same time the most comprehensive symbol for the calamity of the *conditio humana*. In two choral dramas for National Socialist celebrations, *Death and Life* and *The Greatness of Creation*, published together under the title of *The Triumph of Life*, Schumann records the movements of the soul from its protest against death to its finding redemption; the soul's journey expresses the particular nature of its faith.

In the mystery play *Death and Life* the anonymous figure of "the man" struggles against the allegorical figure of death. In danger of being defeated, his "comrades" gather around him. But one after another as they come into contact with death they perish, until finally "the choir of the dead" comes to the aid of the living and takes up the flag that has been passed from hand to hand.

32 Ibid.

33 Hanns Johst, *Ich glaube! Bekenntnisse* (Munich 1928) 36, 73–75. See "Introduction," 11.

When one of us falls
The next silently takes his place.
If we all fall, our blood
still waves in the fiber of the flag
And continues to sire.[34]

There is more at stake here than ideology. The existential depth of motivation is revealed in the metaphors: "Like a tower this faith rises from my soul./ Have I not carried an upright will before me like a flag?" When the flag stands, "the man stands in the sun's streams of lust" and "mates in the breath of flame."[35] It would be too easy to conclude that these images reveal the youthful author's projection of sexual desire into National Socialism in an attempt to sublimate and repress it. The sexually charged images express a longing that goes beyond sexuality. Here is neither a clever propaganda for ideological content, nor a sublimated reaction to sexual impulses, but, as the title of the work indicates, a concern with life and death. That is to say, the work confronts central questions of existence: how, in the face of death can life assert itself, or—to the extent that here death is to be understood symbolically—how is redemption to be won out of the predicament of creatureliness? The images of phallic erection, like those of religious fervor, are the most intensive expressions of the vital will, the desperate longing to overcome death, and an index of redemption: "As the staff points to heaven [...] so the flag awakens the dead."[36] The unity of religious and sexual excitement reveals that the solution the author has found is of the highest existential importance.

The flag as the symbol of "victorious life" represents National Socialism. For Schumann National Socialism is not just an ideology and a political movement but ultimately a power that promises redemption, in other words it conquers death. But what is the basis of this faith? The answer offered by National Socialism is thin––namely, it means to live on in one's descendents, i.e., in "biological immortality." In a National Socialist marriage ceremony "cantata" the "closing choral" speaks these lines:

34 Gerhard Schumann, *Siegendes Leben. Dichtungen für eine Gemeinschaft* (Oldenburg and Berlin: Stalling, 1935), 27.
35 Ibid., 10f., 13.
36 Ibid., 25.

Keep our blood pure,
That its red strength
And sacred virtue
May course through the living blood
down to the furthest generation.[37]

But for each individual facing death biological immortality is a rather cold comfort and the individual ego must seek redemption in other ways, finally finding it in the act of sacrifice. Yet since sacrifice means death for the individual it is a paradoxical solution for the individual. And in order to justify it Schumann can only point to life "as such." Although, naturally, the goal of "biological immortality" does not provide a logical reason for the necessity of an individual to sacrifice his life:

Life lives because he who spends it
Loves the flying flag more than he loves himself.
The tempestuous life that never ends,
As long as one sacrifices himself.[38]

It is obvious that here the material justification is not important; rather it is the willingness to sacrifice that gives the individual the *feeling* of redemption. And this feeling comes about in a particular way in that the willingness to sacrifice is actualized, for example in the individual's self-surrender. The dissolution of the self, that frees the individual of weaknesses and limitations, is experienced as lustful joy. The phallic images in which the desire to be fully alive is presented, and which at first seem to express the individual's own life-will, merge repeatedly with images of consecration and of "spending oneself" in "radiant release and sublimation (*strahlendes Entschweben*)."[39] In *The Greatness of Creation*, which was broadcast over all German radio stations on June 23, 1935, as the morning celebration of the HJ, the images of the dissolution of the individual, the breaking of all

37 Gerhard Schumann, *Die heilige Stunde. Kantate* (Munich: Langen–Müller, 1938), 7.
38 Schumann, *Siegendes Leben*, 27.
39 Ibid., 11.

barriers and flowing into the whole, are even more strongly emphasized: "Flowing together is dissolving, silently losing the self to be taken up in what is Greater"; "You should surge forth like the river surges"; "Give yourself, surrender yourself, let yourself pour forth."[40] These images achieve seductive excitement because they are metaphors of the dissolution of the individual in the act of copulation, as the comparison with one of Schumann's love poems, "Giving" (*Hingebung*) reveals:

> It is no more "I" and "you"—We end,
> giving ourselves to the whole
> In the star spangled fire of our lust.[41]

The desire to give up the self is aesthetically realized in the celebration. The individual, "the man" presented without individual characteristics, is dissolved into the "chorus" of comrades who represent the National Socialist community. Here self-sacrifice is literally a sacrifice of the self. Losing the "I" in this form can be a pleasurable experience like the dissolution in coitus: the dissolution gives one—to quote Johst—an "incomparable feeling of well-being." Denis de Rougemont referred to the new religion of National Socialism as a "lukewarm bath in which the ego that was once sinful and responsible dissolves."[42]

How seriously can we take the "faith" of National Socialists? Enthusiastic young writers like Schumann and Böhme certainly believed what they wrote; the extremely emotional register of their language came, so to speak "from the heart" and was not feigned. And without a doubt there was the SS member or member of the HJ who believed and was ready to sacrifice his life for the *Fuehrer* as late as April 1945. On the other hand, there was also the cynical National Socialist functionary who believed in nothing but power, or the technocratic administrator whose soul only responded to the mechanism of command and obedience. It is more difficult to answer the question of the earnestness of the faith of propagandists, from head propa-

40 Ibid., 34, 43, 45.

41 Gerhard Schumann, *Wir dürfen dienen. Gedichte* (Munich: Langen-Müller, 1937), 58.

42 De Rougemont, *Journal aus Deutschland 1935–1936*, 69.

gandist Goebbels to people like Eugen Hadamovsky, or even Hanns Johst. But I think that their propagandistic spreading of the ideas of National Socialist faith does not necessarily stand in contradiction to their own beliefs. Propaganda and faith are not opposites. This was true of Hitler himself who certainly until the end of his life believed that the Jews were the "evil enemy of mankind."[43] Rüdiger Safranski summarized brilliantly the co-existence of demagogic propaganda and faith in Hitler: "[He] unscrupulously used any demagogic means. And in *Mein Kampf* he expressly justified using lies as a means to helping a higher purpose to success. In his mind this purpose—the delusional system of Anti-Semitism and its practical realization in genocide—was not a tissue of lies. He believed in it and made others believe in it and produced the willingness to commit murder."[44]

43 Hitler, *Mein Kampf*, 724.

44 Rüdiger Safranski, *Das Böse oder Das Drama der Freiheit* (Frankfurt: Fischer, 9th ed. 2011), 286.

The movement celebrates an hour of devotion as a sea of light repels the outer darkness.

Roll Call of the political leaders on September 10, 1937. *Niederelbisches Tageblatt* [A daily newspaper]

CHAPTER 3

MYSTICSIM

Contemporary writers of various persuasions used the concept of mysticism to describe National Socialism. At the end of 1933 the Austrian psychoanalyst Wilhelm Reich, living in Berlin since 1930, published *The Mass Psychology of Fascism* in which he underlined the importance of sexual issues in the political movement. Reich was not only a psychoanalyst but also a Marxist, and in both cases deviated from "pure doctrine." In 1934 he was expelled from the International Psychoanalytic Association. A year earlier he had been expelled from the German Communist Party (KPD), primarily for *The Mass Psychology of Fascism* in which he criticized Marxism's socio-economic model for being unable to interpret certain phenomena of National Socialism and, above all, for being unable to explain its success. He observed "defects in the Marxist grasp of reality" which prevented it from being able to explain why "in a profound crisis of poverty and suffering National Socialist mysticism could triumph over scientific socialism."[1]

Denis de Rougemont, who in 1935–1936 was a lecturer at the University of Frankfurt am Main,[2] wrote in his diary that National Socialist ideology articulates itself as a "religion of the nation and the race," or as a "religion of soil and blood." More than once he described National Socialist religion as "mysticism" because above all it responded to the people's longing "for a principle of unity."[3]

As we pointed out above,[4] in 1938 Erich Voegelin interpreted Nazism as a "political religion." This insight was based, among other things, on

1 Wilhelm Reich, *Massenpsychologie des Faschismus. Zur Sexualökonomie der politischen Reaktion und zur proletarischen Sexualpolitik* (Kopenhagen, Prag, Zurich: Verlag für Sexual-Politik,1933), 16.

2 See above, chapter 2.

3 Denis de Rougemont, *Journal d'Allemagne.* Here quoted according to the German edition, *Journal aus Deutschland 1935–1936*, 88, 91, 94 ("Schlußfolgerungen 1938"), 107–119, 124 ("Postskriptum 1939").

4 See above, chapter 2.

what Voegelin recognized to be "religious agitation" in the believers' "ecstasy of the deed," and he therefore called such vitalist ecstasies "acts of mystical self-dissolution."[5]

The authors we have just cited who attributed a mystical quality to National Socialism did so under the auspices of various philosophical and political positions. However all of them used the terms "mystic" or "mystical" not just descriptively, but critically. The National Socialist leaders themselves differed on what they thought about the "mystical." Goebbels had a weakness for solemn ceremonies (which he also organized) and a tendency to express emotion enthusiastically. On the roll call of the SA at the 1937 Reich Party Congress he noted in his diary: "An almost religious ceremony [...]. The consecration of new flags takes place in an air of wondrous mystical enchantment,"[6] Hitler had invented the ceremony of consecrating the new standards by bringing them into contact with the "Martyrs' Flag" of 1923,[7] but he rejected some other forms of National Socialist "mysticism" and used the term "mystic" in a derogatory sense in order to distance himself from it. In this way he could defend himself against opponents' criticism and, even more importantly, against particular mystical tendencies in the Party.

Among the prominent Nazi leaders, Himmler and Rosenberg were especially inclined to mysticism. In his memoirs Albert Speer wrote of an afternoon discussion while taking tea at Obersalzberg in which Hitler talked about Himmler's notions of the SS as a spiritual order: "What nonsense! We have finally entered an age that has overcome mysticism and he wants to start again from scratch. We might as well have stayed in the church."[8] And in a major speech at the Reich Party Congress in 1938 Hitler proclaimed: "There were eras in which semi-darkness was necessary for certain teachings to become effective; now we live in an age when light is the fundamental condition for the success of action. It will be a sorry day when *dark mystical elements creep into the movement* or the state and begin to issue

5 Eric Voegelin, *The Collected Works*, vol. 5, 68f.

6 Fröhlich, *Die Tagebücher von Joseph Geobbles*, Part I, vol. 4.

7 See below pages 65–66 and the photo on page 78.

8 Albert Speer, *Erinnerungen* (Berlin: Propyläen-Verlag, 1969), 108.

their murky orders! And that sad day will be at hand the moment our language becomes obscure."[9]

Yet although Hitler rejected "mysticism" and amused himself at the expense of Himmler and Rosenberg,[10] he let them continue their activities unabated. Of course, Himmler was a force to be reckoned with. Immediately after coming to power in 1933 the *Reichsführer SS* had learned only too well how to consolidate his power and to steadily increase it. But he was careful to keep his all too esoteric and occult notions to himself in order not to embarrass Hitler or offend the public.[11] Rosenberg's case was different. In the NSDAP he was regarded as a kind of chief ideological authority. In 1921 he became editor and chief of the Party newspaper, *The Peoples' Observer* (publishing editor in 1938). In 1934 Hitler appointed him the "*Fuehrer's* Commissioner for Monitoring the Entire Spiritual and Ideological Education and Training of the NSDAP." But the high sounding title brought nothing like the powers that, for example, Himmler had. Still Rosenberg represented the "folkish" fraction of the Party and exercised considerable influence in ideological matters. Hitler himself rejected the folk-movement with its longing for so-called Teutonic and neo-pagan religiosity. As far back as *Mein Kampf* he had made fun of the "German wandering scholars" who "prattle about the Teutonic heroism of a fog enshrouded past, and of stone axes, battle spears, and shields."[12] At the 1934 Reich Party Congress he again sharply criticized backward-looking *Volk*ish individuals.[13] But he needed their support in the struggle for power and Rosenberg reflected their interests. Beyond this Rosenberg was an important

9 *Der Parteitag Großdeutschland vom 5–12. September 1938.* Offizieller Bericht über den Verlauf des Parteitages mit sämtlichen Kongreßreden (Munich: Eher 1938), 81–82. (Italics in the original).

10 Speer, *Erinnerungen*, 109; Reinhard Bollmus, *Das Amt Rosenberg und seine Gegner. Studien zum Machtkampf im nationalsozialistischen Herrschaftssystem* (Stuttgart: Deutsche Verlags-Anstalt, 1970), 17–18.

11 Peter Longerich, *Heinrich Himmler. Biographie* (Munich: Pantheon, 2010), 265–308.

12 Adolf Hitler, *Mein Kampf*, 395–396.

13 *Der Kongreß zu Nürnberg vom 5. bis 10. September 1934*. Offizieller Bericht über den Verlauf des Reichsparteitages mit sämtlichen Reden (Munich: Eher, 1934), 103.

propagandist of racial Anti-Semitism, and on this point there were no ideological differences between Hitler and Rosenberg. The ideology of his book, *The Myth of the 20th Century*, published in 1930, provided one of the leading justifications for subsequent National Socialist racial policy. As Speer noted, publically the book was widely regarded as the standard work on Party ideology.[14] It had an official rank in the Party and was used in its training courses. By 1945 over one million copies were in circulation.[15]

Hitler expressed his reservations concerning *The Myth of the 20th Century*, but only to his intimate circle and not to Rosenberg himself. As Albert Speer wrote, Hitler described the book "curtly as 'stuff no one can understand' written by a 'narrow minded *Balt* who thinks in a horribly convoluted way.'" Hitler was surprised "'that a book like that could have such an enormous circulation: A throwback to medieval notions!'"[16] But for the outer world Hitler stood by his Commissioner for Monitoring the Entire Spiritual and Ideological Education and Training of the NSDAP and in 1937 Rosenberg was among the first to be awarded the National Prize for Art and Science, Hitler's substitute for the Nobel Prize and created as a reaction to the awarding of that prize to Carl von Ossietzky.[17] Goebbels noted in his diary: "The *Fuehrer's* opinion on the National Prize: Rosenberg, Sauerbruch, and Furtwängler. A strange trio. Rosenberg simply doesn't belong in it. But the *Fuehrer* wants to put a band-aid on his wounds of unfulfilled ambition."[18]

14 Speer, *Erinnerungen*, 110.

15 Cf. Bollmus, *Das Amt Rosenberg und seine Gegner*, Claus-Ekkehard Bärsch, *Die politische Religion des Nationalsozialismus. Die religiösen Dimensionen der NS-Ideologie in den Schriften von Dietrich Eckart, Joseph Goebbels, Alfred Rosenberg und Adolf Hitler* (Munich: Fink 2002), esp. 197 seq.; Ernst Piper, *Alfred Rosenberg: Hitlers Chefideologe* (Munich: Pantheon, 2005); for the reactions to Rosenberg's book, see esp. 212–213.

16 Speer, *Erinnerungen*, 110.

17 Hitler's decree was made public by Hermann Göring in the Reichstag on January 30, 1937: "In order to prevent such shameless occurrences in the future, I have today created a German National Prize for Art and Science. [...] With this decree the acceptance of Nobel Prizes in the future is forbidden to Germans." Quoted in Carl von Ossietzky, *Sämtliche Schriften*, vol. VII: *Briefe und Lebensdokumente* (Reinbek: Rowohlt, 1994), 840–841.

18 Frölich, *Die Tagebücher von Joseph Goebbels*, Part I, vol. 4, 293 (September 3, 1937). As a matter of fact Rosenberg was awarded the prize, along with the

The ideology of race in Rosenberg's *Myth of the 20th Century* is linked to mystical ideas in a curious way. This mysticism was only one variety of National Socialist religiousness, but because it was Rosenberg's it represented an important part of the Party's politico-religious spectrum. The book's concept of human races has little to do with the biological and genetic theories of the 1920s. For example, it does not mention Fritz Lenz[19] and Walter Scheidt;[20] and Hans Friedrich Karl Günther,[21] whose *Rassenkunde des Deutschen Volkes* (1922) and numerous other works on race had a significant influence on racial courses taught at universities, and after 1933 on the political doctrine of race, is dismissed in a footnote as not being "very important regarding the essence of the matter."[22] Rosenberg's concept of race is primarily cultural and spiritual. Although the notion of blood plays an important role in it, the term does not designate a biological substance but a myth.[23] In Rosenberg's eyes world history is determined by the fundamental difference between the Nordic race and the Jewish counter-race, and these differences are rooted in cultural and ultimately religious qualities. His chief witness for the essence of the Nordic race is the mystic Meister Eckhart (Rosenberg prefers the spelling "Eckehart") whom he calls the "greatest apostle of the Nordic

surgeons Ferdinand Sauerbruch and August Bier, the explorer Wilhelm Filcher, and, posthumously, "the *Fuehrer's* architect" Paul Ludwig Troost who died in 1934.

19 Medical doctor, student of the race theorist Alfred Ploetz, 1923, the first Professor for Racial Hygiene at the University of Munich, 1913–1933 editor of the "Archiv für Rassen und Gesellschaftsbiologie," 1933 Professor of Eugenics at the University of Berlin, and director of the section Human Heredity, Racial Hygiene, and Eugenics at the Kaiser Wilhelm-Institute for Anthropology.

20 In 1928 Professor of Anthropology at the University of Hamburg. Major works: *Allgemeine Rassenkunde* (1925), *Kulturbiologie* (1930).

21 1930 Professor of Social Anthropology at the University of Jena, 1935 at the University of Berlin and Director of the *Anstalt für Rassenkunde und Völkerbiologie* (Berlin); 1940–45 Professor at the University of Freiburg.

22 Alfred Rosenberg, *Der Mythus des 20. Jahrhunderts. Eine Wertung der seelisch-geistigen Gestaltenkämpfe unserer Zeit* (Munich: Hoheneichen, 17–29th ed., 1934 [first edition 1930]), 86.

23 Ibid., 216.

occident."[24] An entire chapter is devoted to him because Rosenberg views him as the "creator of a new religion, our religion"[25] and believes that Meister Eckhart's spirit was the dawn of "a new era of German mysticism."[26]

One might well ask: what does race have to do with mysticism and, in particular, with Meister Eckhart's? I will first sketch Rosenberg's interpretation, without immediately commenting on it. Rosenberg begins with the heart of Meister Eckhart's mystical experience, the *unio mystica*, but interprets the finding of God in "one's own breast" to mean that the self and God are "polarities of the soul."[27] Out of the mystical experience of the "unity with God" Rosenberg asserts the "likeness of the soul with God" and that "God and the soul are equivalent."[28] The next step in his interpretation is the transition from the concepts of polarity and equivalence to the idea that the soul and God are of "equal value"; and Rosenberg vehemently protests against the "apparently ineradicable notion that the self and God are essentially different."[29] As the quintessence of his Eckhart exegesis he postulates: "The hereditary Nordic spiritual values are rooted in the consciousness, not only of the human soul's *likeness* to God but of its *own godliness*."[30] This consciousness of the identity of the soul with God is the foundation of the "Nordic idea of *self-realization*."[31] This in turn is contrasted with the Jewish idea of God: the transcendent God Yahweh is alien to the human being and prevents the self-realization of the soul. In opposition to the "Satan-Nature" of Judaism, Nordic man is "Luciferian," or creative.[32]

Rosenberg's interpretation of Meister Eckhart tries to demonstrate the individual soul's equality with God, but how does he move from there to a notion of race as a collective entity? For Rosenberg race is just another form in which the soul manifests itself: "Soul is race viewed from within.

24 Ibid., 218.
25 Ibid., 239.
26 Ibid., 216.
27 Ibid., 219, 248.
28 Ibid., 222, 236.
29 Ibid., 223.
30 Ibid., 246 (Italics in the original spaced).
31 Ibid., 248 (Italics in the original spaced).
32 Ibid., 263–265.

Conversely, race is the external side of the soul."[33] He postulates a "racial soul" that manifests itself in the race's exceptional representatives,[34] for example in Eckhart, in Friedrich the Great (whom he calls "Friedrich the incomparable"), in Kant, Goethe, and Beethoven. This is the context in which Rosenberg's concept of blood must be seen. It is a notion of blood as a myth or indeed as a religion.[35] The race-soul expresses itself in the folk "bonded in blood" and it is the blood-myth that gives birth to the consciousness of belonging to a particular race.[36] In the myth of the blood, the people recognize that through the realization of the racial soul—analogous to the experience of the unity of God and man in the individual soul—the soul becomes "at one with itself" and achieves the "totality of life."[37]

In this way Rosenberg projects the vision of the mystical soul onto the "body of the people" (*Volkskörper*). That the racial legitimation of the national community (*Volksgemeinschaft*) was based on a mystical quality was recognized very early in the study of National Socialism. For this reason Eric Voegelin in his 1933 book, *Race and State*, differentiated between the "theory of race" and the "idea of race," viewing the latter as a particular instance of "body ideas" that do not claim to be scientific, but which play a role in creating community and which therefore belong to the realm of practical politics. Whether in fact the distinction between racial theory and racial ideas is meaningful and unambiguous does not concern us here. In this context what is important is Voegelin's insight that body ideas—and therewith the idea of race—"are *never* scientific judgments concerning matters in the biological sphere through which their correctness could be tested; rather, the idea of the community as a body is *always* a 'mythic' idea, and it *always* (not only in the case of the Christian community) establishes a *corpus mysticum*."[38]

33 Ibid., 2.
34 Ibid., 697.
35 Ibid., 258.
36 Ibid., 258, 697.
37 Ibid., 697, 699.
38 Erich Voegelin, *Rasse und Staat* (Tübingen: J. C. B. Mohr [Paul Siebeck], 1933), 14 (Italics in the original). Quoted from *Race and State, The Collected Works of Eric Voegelin*, vol. 2. Edited with an Introduction by Klaus Vondung (Baton Rouge: Louisiana State University Press, 1997), 13.

There is a temptation to agree, for once, with a judgment of Hitler, namely that Rosenberg's *Myth of the 20th Century* is about "stuff" that "no one can understand," and to leave it at that. Nevertheless, it is important to take a closer look at Rosenberg's adaptation of Meister Eckhart's mysticism. In this way we can gain insight into some of the significant differences between genuine mysticism and "mystical derailments"; and most importantly we can uncover some of the motives that led Rosenberg to support his racist world view with mystical elements and see what consequences ensued from race-mysticism.

The essential core of any mystical world view is the idea and the perception of a perfect reality that constitutes the all-encompassing ground of being. This comprises the notion of the unity of all that is real, including the thinking subject's connection with perfect reality.[39] Based on this experience, or intuition, Meister Eckhart explains the act of uniting with the Absolute as entering into the "Ground" of being. However, it is clear that for Eckhart this does not imply a pantheistic or monistic equating of the knowing subject with the Absolute. Nor does it mean that the Absolute, or God, is identical with the center of the soul that experiences the Absolute. It is not the entire soul, but only a part of the soul, a "spark," that is "like God."[40] But what does Rosenberg do with this idea? First he transforms the complex structure of Eckhart's exegesis of the tension between entities of reality and the perfect reality, and between the subject and the Absolute, into a model in which the ego and God are the soul's polarities. Then he dissolves the polarity between identity and non-identity by asserting a further identity that overrides both—a step that amounts to equating the human soul with God.[41]

39 The argument that follows is based on the research of Christian Steineck, *Grundstrukturen mystischen Denkens* (Würzburg: Königshausen and Neumann, 2000); Alois M. Haas, *Mystik im Kontext* (Munich: Fink, 2004); Karl Albert, *Einführung in die philosophische Mystik* (Darmstadt: Wissenschaftliche Buchgesellschaft, 1996). For Meister Eckhart: Joachim Kopper, *Die Metaphysik Meister Eckharts* (Saarbrücken: West – Ost – Verlag, 1955); Erwin Waldschütz, *Denken und Erfahren des Grundes. Zur philosophischen Deutung Meister Eckharts* (Vienna: Herder, 1989).

40 Meister Eckehart, *Deutsche Predigten und Traktate*. Edited and Translated by Josef Quint (Zurich: Diogenes 1979), 164, 427; see also Steineck, *Grundstrukturen mystischen Denkens*,43, 69 seq.

41 See also Bärsch, *Die Politische Religion des Nationalsozialismus*, 242 seq.

This is clearly a crude misinterpretation of Meister Eckhart (not to mention the extrapolation of the individual soul into a race soul and turning Eckhart into a representative of the Nordic race). It is safe to say that Rosenberg's construction is of no theoretical value. Thus in *Race and State* Voegelin confined himself to the brief remark that Rosenberg opposed "a concept of organic truth to that of scientific truth."[42] Ultimately, however, it is not enough to simply establish the fact that "race ideas" have a community building function. For, naturally, the argument of political ideas and their adequacy or inadequacy to articulate reality can also be objects of critical analysis. And Rosenberg, with his claim of supporting a "world view" with an exegesis of Eckhart's writings, invites such analysis. Indeed we must point to a further derailment in his interpretation.

Theoretically this is the decisive criticism: Rosenberg reifies symbols that Meister Eckhart used to express the meaning of his mystical experience, i. e. he treats symbols that point neither to entities in the space-time continuum nor to objects of knowledge as though they were "things." But Meister Eckhart was not only a mystic, he was also a skilled theoretician and for him mystical experience did not exclude the pursuit of knowledge and the use of rational argument; if it had, he would not have interpreted his insights and made them known. (This is true of many other mystics too, for example Nicholas of Cusa.) In addition to the view of a perfect reality mentioned above, a further essential characteristic of mysticism is its mode of gaining knowledge. The explication of knowledge gained through the interpretation of mystical experience by no means excludes the use of the rational method but indeed includes it, even as it seeks to transcend it––for example, the concept of unity implies the idea of a "true reality that transcends contradictions; on the one hand this reality includes all determinations, but on the other hand reality as a whole eludes every determining limitation and thereby defies conceptualization."[43] Philosophical mystics like Eckhart and Nicholas of Cusa were aware that words are the correlates of the experience of object-reality and seem to designate objects, but that the true and perfect reality experienced by the mystic is not an "object" and therefore cannot be "grasped" by concepts. This insight leads to a third

42 Voegelin, *Race and State*, 14.

43 Steineck, *Grundstrukturen mystischen Denkens*, 261.

essential characteristic of mysticism, namely to a specific mode of linguistic explication. Although mystical experience is principally ineffable, the mystic attempts to convey the experience in language. But, naturally, in view of the objectifying function of concepts, the mystic also tries to demonstrate the distance between his experience and the language in which he interprets it. He does this by using metaphors and neologisms and by speaking in paradoxes. It is an attempt to point to the higher truth of perfect reality—to the truth that transcends all the worldly opposites that are present in rational thought. For example, Meister Eckhart's metaphor of the "spark," for the part of the soul that is God-like, must be understood as both a symbol for the *sensorium* and as an image of the experience of the *unio mystica* itself, and not be taken for a thing. For ultimately the *sensorium* that is illuminated in the experience "cannot be expressed by any name and is without form."[44] Rosenberg misreads symbols like spark, unity, God, and God-likeness as entities that can be determined and realized existentially and socially. How does he arrive at this notion, and what does it imply? The reification of these symbols makes it easy for him to postulate for the human soul an "equality with God" (or God-likeness) and thus deifies the human being. In this way self realization is turned into self-redemption through self-deification. Then self-redemption of the divinized individual proceeds by means of the construed race soul to the self-salvation of a people made up of such individuals. And the people that manifests itself in the race soul is said to achieve a "life totality" (*Lebenstotalität*) and divine perfection.

"But what does becoming God mean?" Albert Camus asked. He answered: "It means, in fact, recognizing that everything is permitted, and refusing to recognize any other law but one's own."[45] Hopefully, it will now have become clear what function Meister Eckhart's mysticism has in Rosenberg's argumentation and with what intention Rosenberg tries to move beyond Eckhart. The experience of the *unio mystica* with God is reinterpreted to mean that the human being is equal to God. And according to Rosenberg, from this reinterpretation it follows that "today an iron will [must

44 Meister Eckehart, *Deutsche Predigten und Traktate*, 163.
45 Albert Camus, *The Rebel: An Essay on Man in Revolt* (New York: Vintage Books, 1956), 58–59.

be] joined to Eckhart's insights that is courageous and strong enough to draw *all* the consequences contained in his knowledge."[46] The first of these consequences is the assumption of the Nordic human being's equality with God (*Gottgleichheit*) and the assertion of his "Luciferian nature." The further consequence is the demand that the Nordic human being consciously develop his Luciferian creativity and apply it practically. For this reason the chapter on this subject in *The Myth of the Twentieth Century* is titled, "Mysticism and Action." But, as Camus pointed out, the acts of human beings who have deified themselves are subject to no law but their own.

Still, Rosenberg never explains just how the transition from mysticism to action is to take place and says nothing about it in his race ideology. Thus, at the Nuremberg Tribunal, with regard to the question of his complicity in acts of genocide, he is able to say: "[My] conscience is completely clear." Those responsible for the murder of the Jews, far from being his comrades, were his foes: "I must declare that their sinister deeds were not the implementation of the National Socialism for which millions of faithful men and women fought, but a shameful betrayal, degenerate acts which I roundly condemn."[47]

It is true that Rosenberg had no direct organizational responsibility for the systematic murder of Jews in death camps, but he knew about it and he bears political responsibility for it. In 1941 Rosenberg was appointed Reich Minister for the Occupied Eastern Territories. Two of his most important collaborators were present at the Wannsee Conference on January 20th, 1942, where the "Final Solution" to the "Jewish Question" was planned. Massacres by the *Einsatzgruppen* ("task forces"), raising of ghettos, and deportations to death camps took place in his region of responsibility. That is why he was condemned to death at the Nuremberg Tribunal.[48] But his role as the chief ideologue of the NSDAP and therefore his intellectual and moral responsibility weigh even heavier than his political responsibility. He had provided the faithful National Socialists that he referred to during the Nuremberg trial with doctrines that denounced Jews as the "world's

46 Rosenberg, *Der Mythus des 20. Jahrhunderts*, 218 (Italics in the original).

47 Joe Heydecker and Johannes Leeb, *Der Nürnberger Prozeß* (Cologne: Kiepenheuer and Witsch, 1979), 458.

48 See also Piper, *Alfred Rosenberg*, 632–635.

criminals" and had claimed that "World-Jewry" was preparing for a "world-wide struggle" against the Nordic race.[49] At the 1936 Reich Party Congress Rosenberg declared that the threat of this "world struggle" could only be opposed successfully "by a new *faith*" and "by a will to action born out of this *Weltanschauung* and *finally* through the decisive act itself."[50] In 1936 the murder of the European Jews was not yet on the political horizon, but for the self-deified Luciferian man who was a law unto himself every act had now become possible.

49 Alfred Rosenberg, *Der entscheidende Weltkampf. Rede des Reichsleiters Alfred Rosenberg auf dem Parteikongreß in Nürnberg 1936* (Munich, n.d. [1936]), 2, 16.
50 Ibid., 13 (Italics in the original spaced).

He who follows this flag salutes its cloth
As he would hail God in his sanctuary,
Who had called him to serve;
On these steps blood's muffled drum
Beats the tattoo of fame.

Herbert Böhme, *Cantata For the 9th of November.*

CHAPTER 4

MYTH AND RITUAL

The title of Rosenberg's major work shows that the term "myth" (he used the form "Mythus") was a central concept in his world view. But although the work speaks constantly of myth it never really defines it. Rosenberg writes of a "myth of the blood" and of "the soul,"[1] and since the "mysticism of the racial soul" is the obvious center of his ideology, one can safely assume that for him myth means something like an intuitively grasped idea or a truth of faith. But, in any case, his myth is not like the myths of Hesiod's *Theogony*, Homer's *Iliad*, or Ovid's *Metamorphoses*—narratives of the creation of the world, of gods and human beings, and of the stirring acts of demigods and heroes. Nor is it like the political myths that are cultivated in modern national States. In general the "national myths,"[2] most of which were created in the 19th century or became publicly effective at that time, transfigure fundamental events, such as the shots fired at Lexington, Massachusetts, that initiated the American Revolution, or the storming of the Bastille that sparked the French Revolution, or the battle in Teutoburg forest in Germany against the Romans, or the battle of Sedan against the French and the proclamation of the German Empire in 1871. National myths take up an historical event and transform it to create meaning, strengthen national self-esteem, and call the nation to unity.

In our study we are confronted with the paradox that, on the one hand, Alfred Rosenberg who constantly spoke of myth never narrated any of this type, and on the other hand, that a myth similar to the "myths of the nation," and in some respects much like ancient myths, played an important role in the Third Reich even though it was not referred to as a myth. This is the myth of the 9th of November which narrates Hitler's 1923 putsch attempt in Munich and re-works the event in a manner reminiscent of national myths.

1 Alfred Rosenberg, *Der Mythus des 20. Jahrhunderts*, 258, 699.

2 *Mythen der Nationen. Ein europäisches Panorama* ed. Monika Flacke. Ausstellungskatalog. Deutsches Historisches Museum (Berlin, 1998); Cf. also Herfried Münkler, *Die Deutschen und ihre Mythen* (Berlin: Rowohlt, 2009).

Before I discuss its contents and analyze the role it played in the National Socialist movement and State, I will briefly recount the historical facts. On November 8, 1923, at a meeting of anti-republican forces at the Bürgerbräu Beer Hall in Munich, Hitler proclaimed the beginning of a national revolution. On November 9th, Hitler and World War I's General Ludendorff led a demonstration of SA and members of the paramilitary organization Bund Oberland through Munich with the intention of carrying out a putsch. Most of the demonstrators were armed. At the Feldherrnhalle (a monumental loggia to the Bavarian army) the police barred the marchers' path and a short but sharp exchange of fire took place in which fourteen demonstrators and four policemen were killed. Hitler fled. Two hours later in a brief skirmish in the courtyard of the former War Ministry that had been occupied by the SA under Ernst Roehm two more rebels were killed. At the 1924 trial for high treason against the organizers of the attempted putsch, Ludendorff was acquitted and Hitler was sentenced to five years imprisonment but released after only eight months. For the time being, the national revolution had failed and thus, in 1932, Theodor Heuss[3] could still write that the putsch retained an "element of the grotesque; at best a melodrama that was booed by its contemporaries."[4]

But in the midst of this fiasco Hitler immediately went to work to turn the failed putsch into a myth. On the first page of volume one of *Mein Kampf*, written during his imprisonment, he listed the sixteen demonstrators who had been killed and introduced their names with the sentence: "On November 9, 1923, at 12:30 in the afternoon, before the Feldherrnhalle and in the courtyard of the former War Ministry in Munich, the following men fell believing loyally in the resurrection of their people." The list of names is followed by the words: "Therefore I dedicate the first volume of this work to them and their collective memory. As the Movement's martyrs may they remain our enduring and guiding light."[5]

3 After World War II he was the first president of the newly founded Federal Republic of Germany (1949–1959).

4 Theodor Heuss, *Hitlers Weg. Eine historisch-politische Studie über den Nationalsozialismus* (Stuttgart, Berlin, Leipzig: Union, 1932), 1.

5 Adolf Hitler, *Mein Kampf*, xxix.

These were the fundamental elements of the myth: the rebels who had been killed were "martyrs" and their deaths a sacred sacrifice for the political goal of the people's "resurrection". Hitler invented this myth. And the highly stylized language of the dedication — the use of the ceremonial "im *Hofe* (instead of *im Hof*) and *zu München* (instead of *in München*), and especially the religious vocabulary—faith, martyrs, and resurrection—served the purpose of mythologizing a historical event and indicates the direction in which the myth could be further developed.

How does a myth gain acceptance? How does it capture the minds, or better, the hearts of so many people? Since a myth's meaning is manifested in ritual, it must be celebrated in ever new ways. This is the way myth worked in the cosmological societies of the ancient world.[6] The national myths of the 19th century likewise became effective by being turned into rituals.[7] The purpose of ritual is not to remind one of a mythically told salvational event, but to re-create the event in the present. Through constant repetition and ever new actualizations salvational events are brought into each respective present as part of its reality. It is clear that early in his career Hitler demonstrated a keen awareness of the importance of ritual.

At the NSDAP's Second Reich Party Congress in Weimar in 1926, the flag with the swastika symbol that had been carried on the march to the Feldherrnhalle was consecrated in a special ceremony and elevated to the status of a sacred relic. At the general roll call of the SA and SS in the Weimar National Theater, Hitler consecrated eight new flags by touching their cloth to the "Martyrs' Banner"(*Blutfahne*, literally the "Blood Flag").[8] The purpose of the ritual was the magical transmission of power and, as the following lines of Hans Baumann show, that was how it was understood:

6 Cf. Ernst Cassirer, *Philosophie der symbolischen Formen. Zweiter Teil: Das mythische Denken* (Darmstadt:Wissenschaftliche Buchgesellschaft, 1973), 50f., 262f.; Mircea Eliade, *Das Heilige und das Profane: Vom Wesen des Religiösen* (Hamburg: Rowohlt, 1957), 56–62.

7 Cf. Etienne Francois und Hagen Schulze, "Das emotionale Fundament der Nationen," in ed. Flacke, *Mythen der Nationen*, vol. 1, 19.

8 That the city of Weimar let the NSDAP use the National Theater for its anti-Republican ceremony, the same building in which the constitution of the German Republic had been adopted following World War One, reveals a great deal about the nature of the city's spirit.

Let your hands grasp
These flag masts with pride,
For they are imbued with the strength
Of the One [incomparable] flag.[9]

In all subsequent Reich Party Congresses Hitler repeated the consecration of new Party flags by holding them to the Blutfahne. The ritual can be seen in Leni Riefenstahl's film of the 1934 Reich Party Congress, "Triumph of the Will". Only at Party Congresses and November 9th commemorations was the Blutfahne displayed publically, a fact that emphasized its status as a sacred relic.

After 1933 the observation of the myth of the 9th of November was expanded. As we noted, up to that time the putsch had been regarded as a fiasco and in the long run without overcoming the defeat it did not have much value as a myth. Therefore, only when Hitler actually became Chancellor on January 30th, 1933, and the NSDAP extended its rule throughout Germany, could the myth's claim to embody truth gain acceptance and the ritual become effective. The 30th of January, 1933, "proved" that the apparently futile 1923 putsch was in fact a "sacred event" and that what had been revealed at that time had now become reality. In 1933 the myth seemed to demonstrate that National Socialism's victory had been prefigured by the sacrificial deaths of 1923: the "blood sacrifice" had not only created the conditions for the later triumph but had borne the seeds of victory. Hitler''s coming to power, the actual political success, was viewed as a second "sacred event" which fulfilled the first revelation, the 9th of November's vision of German "resurrection". Thus in 1933 the myth was said to narrate National Socialist "sacred history".

The 9th of November had a special place in the Third Reich's Annual National Socialist Celebrations. "Remembrance Day for Those Who gave Their Lives for the Movement," as the day was officially designated, was the most solemn holiday in the National Socialist calendar. On no other occasion was there so much ritual celebration and the speeches and reports of that day's individual events were also mythical commentaries suffused with religious terms and symbols. At the center of the ritual was the

9 Hans Baumann, *Wir zünden das Feuer* (Jena: Diederichs, 1936), 50.

reenactment of the events of 1923, the march of the *Alten Kämpfer* (Old Fighters) from the Bürgerbräukeller to the Feldherrnhalle. In 1935 the celebration reached the height of somber and solemn grandeur, for in that year on the eve of Remembrance Day the exhumed bodies of the sixteen martyrs lay in state in the *Feldherrnhalle*. On November 9th they were transferred to the newly built pantheon (*Ehrentempel*), the Eternal Guard (*Ewige Wache*), at Königsplatz. I will describe the course of this ceremony in order to demonstrate its ritual function and mythical significance.

As darkness fell on the eve of November 9th, Hitler was driven through the Victory Gate (*Siegestor*) toward Odeonsplatz down Ludwig Street that was sparsely decorated with flaming pylons. When he arrived at Odeonsplatz he mounted the steps of the *Feldherrnhalle* to the sarcophagi of his martyrs and stood among them in silent meditation. The mystical commentary of the event was supplied by Herbert Böhme in his *Cantata For the 9th of November*:

> *Fuehrer*, as you strode from this hallowed hall,
> Night's shadow fell from you
> because you carried the torch to the steps of death:
> Lead us in our faith toward light,
> Let the stones tremble under the power of your step.[10]

The mythical image evoked in these verses recalls the shaman who journeys to the realm of the dead and returns with sacred knowledge, or indeed Christ who descended into hell and rose from the dead in order to bring salvation.

The Remembrance Day ritual outlined in these verses also evokes other Christian associations; the liturgy of Good Friday, passion plays, and the procession of Corpus Christi. Late in the morning members of the traditional march column assembled at the *Bürgerbräukeller* dressed as they had been in 1923. Hitler had created an "Order of the Blood" that was awarded to all survivors of the putsch. Ahead of the *Alten Kämpfer* with their Blood Order marched the "Leaders Group" with the *Blutfahne*.

10 Herbert Böhme, *Gesänge unter der Fahne: Vier Kantaten* (Munich: Eher, 1935), 48.

Behind the *Alten Kämpfer* came other important Party members. The route to the *Feldherrnhalle* was flanked by forty pylons, each bearing the name of one of those who had fallen for the Movement. When the march came even with a pylon, the name of the fallen Party member it represented was called out. Loud speakers played the "Horst Wessel Song" and when the column reached the *Feldherrnhalle* it was saluted by sixteen cannon shots, recalling the sixteen deadly volleys of 1923. While Hitler laid a wreath at the plaque honoring the dead the coffins were placed on caissons, "The Good Comrade" was sung followed by the German National Anthem that grew in volume as the column approached Königsplatz where the coffins were placed in the Temples of Honor. A last roll call was taken and as one after another the names of the sixteen martyrs were called out, the assembled members of the Hitler-Youth called back in chorus: "Present!" The calling of each name was followed by a three gun salute, the "Horst Wessel Song" was played, and the coffin was carried to one of the two Temples of Honor. In his speech Hitler interpreted the event: the Martyrs of the Movement had now become Germany's Eternal Guard. The ceremony closed with the "Badenweiler March" followed by the German National Anthem played through loud speakers at full volume.[11]

Through language and ritual the myth of November 9th was turned into a sacred history and its various components took on the aura of the holy. It began with Hitler dedicating *Mein Kampf* to the Movement's martyrs and elevating the *Blutfahne* to the status of a relic that imparted spiritual strength. The process was continued after 1933; and particularly the Feldherrnhalle, the place where the martyrs had fallen, became the sacred place at the heart of the myth. This transformation to the sacred took place through the Remembrance Day ritual and the speeches that interpreted it. Reflecting on the martyrs in his *Cantata For the 9th of November*, Herbert Boehme declared:

11 Description of the event and quotations: "Völkischer Beobachter," 10/11/1935; on the ceremony in the following year: *Zum 9. November 1936*, edited by the NSDAP, Traditionsgau München-Obb. (Munich: Eher, n.d. [1936]); *Vorläufiges Programm für den 8./9. November 1937*. Der Chef des SS-HA. Mikrofilmarchiv des Instituts für Zeitgeschichte. MA-386/4993–4999. For the Remembrance Day ceremony in the years after 1933, see Sabine Behrenbeck, *Der Kult um die toten Helden. Nationalsozialistische Mythen, Riten und Symbole; 1923–1945* (Vierow bei Greifswald: SH – Verlag, 1996), 300.

Now the steps of the Feldherrnhalle are an altar;
Altar, burning mysteriously with their spirit's flame,
And what they were unable to build with their hands,
Stands complete now, built of their blood.[12]

But it was not just the actual architectural structure at Odeonsplatz in Munich that became sacred; the image of the *Feldherrnhalle* itself was turned into a sacred symbol and thus endowed with existential meaning. A choral poem by Gerhard Schumann, appointed by the Culture Division of the Central Party Propaganda Office for Ceremonies Commemorating the 9th November, closes with the verses:

One:
And suddenly before us stands above the teeming
Crowd in its daily work and busy surging haste,
Alone and great against the clearing sky,
The image of the Feldherrnhalle in radiant red light.

All:
We build the Reich's eternal Feldherrnhallen,
the steps to eternity,
And when the hammers fall from our hands
Let us be walled into the altars.[13]

Symbolic quality is attributed to the *Feldherrnhalle* as the image that appears against the background of the "clearing sky." Here sacralization takes place by means of a symbol of revelation that stands for the hierophany, the appearance of the holy. It recalls the baptism of Jesus in The Gospel of Luke and the appearance of the Holy Spirit in the image of the dove in the clearing sky—a symbol depicted in countless works of art.

The *Feldherrnhalle* symbolizes the National Socialist Reich which is said to last eternally. The individual participates in eternity by working until death to build the Reich. Just what this means is expressed a little

12 Böhme, *Gesänge unter der Fahne*, 39.

13 Gerhard Schumann, *Heldische Feier* (Munich: Langen, 1936), 7.

more clearly in the following verses from Böhme's *Cantata For the 9th of November*:

> See, the hall grows toward the firmament,
> Powerful steps climbing toward heaven:
> With your death the old world ended,
> And in your glory our lives begin.[14]

Here the 9th of November is interpreted as a turning point in time through which the old era was virtually brought to an end, and which prefigured the new era that began in 1933. The phrase "our lives begin" refers to the start of a new, transformed, and "essential life" that inaugurates a fundamental change of the social world and human existence. With the end of the "old world" life gains true reality; before this event life was an illusion, as is the life of those who have not yet opened themselves to the new revelation; their lives only seem to be real:

> He lives, who follows your flag,
> and in him live those who died for the flag
> [...]
> For only he is alive who took the sacred oath
> And gave his heart to the Brotherhood:
> Neither want nor death can rob him of anything,
> Joined heart to heart he abides in faith.
> New generations come and the linked chain holds,
> The Reich's flag billows over the grave.[15]

The new life under the swastika flag, consecrated through a vocabulary of the sacred—"faithful" and "holy"—gains a dimension that points beyond temporal existence. The mythical interpretation of the 9th of November also articulates a key existential motive for action: the longing for immortality. In his study of Mao Tse-tung and the Chinese Cultural Revolution, Robert Jay Lifton refers to such longing as the "quest for

14 Böhme, *Gesänge unter der Fahne*, 44.
15 Ibid.

revolutionary immortality."[16] Although Lifton analyzes a different political ideology, indeed one that in many respects is the exact opposite of National Socialism, as far as the psychic attitude of the longing for immortality is concerned the two movements share common ground.[17] In Lifton's view almost every human being is motivated by the need, "in the face of inevitable biological death, to maintain an inner sense of continuity with what has gone on before and what will go on after his own individual existence. From this point of view the sense of immortality is much more than a mere denial of death; it is part of compelling, life-enhancing imagery binding each individual person to significant groups and events removed from him in place and time. It is the individual's inner perception of his involvement in what we call the historical process."[18]

The myth of November 9th provided just such "life enhancing symbolism"; it not only narrated a National Socialist "sacred history" but also promised symbolic immortality. In his choral poem for National Socialist celebrations, Herbert Böhme evokes symbolic immortality in the apocalyptic images that were to define the new era:

Each is ready to answer the SA's call,
the goal, yes the goal of immortality.
What dies in life is dark misery and affliction,
Shining bright above the rosy dawn
Is the *Fuehrer's* flag, the flag.
It glows over the fatherland
And fans the heart's ardent fire.
And the earth stands still.
And also the heavens.
And the Reich is ours,

16 Robert Jay Lifton, *Revolutionary Immortality. Mao Tse-tung and the Chinese Cultural Revolution* (London: Weidenfeld andNicolson, 1968), 7.

17 For a further discussion of the transferability of Lifton's approach and of the modes of "symbolic immortality" see Vondung, *Magie und Manipulation*, 164–170.

18 Lifton, *Revolutionary Immortality*, 7.

Whatever may come,
Ours is the Reich.[19]

The Reich itself also has a symbolic quality and a religious nimbus. The myth tells the story of the martyrs' sacrificial death at the Feldherrnhalle that expresses "German immortality"[20] and establishes the "Eternal Reich."[21] Lifton calls this "sense of immortality" the "creative" one: death is overcome through participation in the creation of a work that survives biological death, in this case the "Eternal Reich."[22]

It is primarily the *Fuehrer's* work that confers immortality. His deed that, so to speak, made him the 9th of November martyr who did not perish, becomes the act of redemption that overcomes death for the "sworn brotherhood" of faithful National Socialists. That the term "redemption" does indeed refer to satisfying the longing for immortality is emphasized in Herbert Böhme's "German Prayer":

You stride among the people as their redeemer,
because faith posses you entirely.
[...]
Here there is no more trembling hesitation:
You say to us: "If you believe,
Then I have slain death, although my body dies.[23]

In addition to the creative mode of symbolic immortality, the myth of the 9th of November also provides a biological one. In his Heroic Celebration of the 9th of November, Gerhard Schumann attributes eternal life to the martyrs using the typical image of transfiguration: "Immortality radiates to the silent dead."[24] The martyrs who gave their blood live forever in

19 Herbert Böhme, *Ruf der SA. Ein Appell mit Liedern* (Munich: Eher, n.d.[1938]), 31.
20 Böhme, *Ruf der SA,* 9.
21 Herbert Böhme, Bekenntnisse *eines jungen Deutschen* (Munich: Eher, 1935), 28.
22 Cf. Lifton, *Revolutionary Immortality*, 7.
23 Herbert Böhme, *Das deutsche Gebet* (Munich: Eher, 1936), 14 f.
24 Schumann, *Heldische Feier*, 5.

National Socialist Man, and he lives eternally in the blood of posterity or--as the Blood and Soil ideology portrays it--lives in the traditional soil as the substantive basis of subsequent generations. The choral oath in Boehme's *Cantata For the 9th of November* reads:

> He who is committed,
> He who took the oath,
> Though he dies or passes away
> Lives on in the land.
>
> He who joins the struggle,
> And keeps its fire in his soul,
> Even when death consumes him,
> Lives on in our blood.[25]

The immortality of the martyrs was expressed concretely in the two Temples of Honor that were erected on Munich's Königsplatz. Programmatically these architectural structures were named the "Eternal Guard." As the martyrs' coffins were placed in the Temples of Honor on November 9th, 1935, Hitler declared in his speech--more a sermon than a speech—that the martyrs' immortality flows into the German people:

> For us they are not dead. This temple is not a grave but an *Eternal Guard*. They stand here for Germany and watch over its people. They lie here as the Movement's faithful witnesses. If, during the time when we were persecuted, we commemorated this day year in and year out, though not always in the same form, and if we are now resolved to commemorate this day hereafter for all time and to consecrate it as a holiday for the German Nation, then not because sixteen men died here. After all thousands of people die every day, and wars consume more men in a single hour. No, we do this because these sixteen men died with truly faithful hearts and in so doing helped the German people rise again.[26]

25 Böhme, *Gesänge unter der Fahne*, 49.
26 Quoted in *DnG*, 1943, 46 (Emphasis in the original).

The immortality of the martyrs who live on in the new National Socialist man was ritually reenacted. As mentioned, at the last roll call at the Eternal Guard the martyrs' names were called out one by one and for each the Hitler Youth responded in chorus "Present!" In this way the resurrection of the sixteen men was symbolized and their eternal life actualized in the "present" of the guardians of the future, who in this way also inherited the martyrs' mantel of immortality. Quite appropriately, the ritual was named "The Celebration of Victory and Resurrection."[27]

Naturally, the symbolic gratification of the longing for immortality had a price. It obliged, primarily the younger generation, to carry on the martyrs' work and, when necessary, to make the same sacrifice. Without a doubt the solemn commemoration of November 9th Remembrance Day had a powerful emotional impact on those who participated in it and, along with other influences, had a lasting effect especially on the young. Particularly, members of the Hitler Youth believed fanatically in the Fuehrer and even in the war's closing days were willing to fight and die for him.

The 9th of November, 1923, was originally a myth of the National Socialist Party. In the Third Reich it became a national myth. In his speech on November 9th, 1935, Hitler underlined his determination to elevate Remembrance Day "to a holiday for the German Nation for all time." But, despite all the efforts through local commemorations and Remembrance Day celebrations in Party organizations, the myth never became firmly anchored in the minds of the people. It was too closely tied to the history and self-understanding of the Party itself, and Remembrance Day was never made into an official State holiday. In addition, there was not enough time before the beginning of the war in 1939 to make it a real part of the people's consciousness and emotions; and once the war began the previously effective public commemorations held in Munich could not be continued on the grand scale of the pre-war years.

27 Cited in the Völkischer Beobachter, November 10, 1935; *Zum 9. November 1936*, ed. by the NSDAP, Traditionsgau München-Obb (Munich: Eher, n.d.[1936]); *Vorläufiges Programm für den 8./9. November 1937.* Der Chef des SS-HA. IfZ, MA-386/4993–4999; *Aufmarschstab für den 8. /9. 11.37 beim Oberabschnitt Süd.*: IfZ, MA-3 86/4977–4984.

Thereafter, the 9th of November was commemorated only locally and in more modest Party ceremonies. Nevertheless, in 1942 as the fortunes of war began to turn against Germany, the National Socialist myth-makers and ceremonial masters renewed their efforts to deepen and expand the meaning of the myth.

The proximity of November 9th to the Sunday of the Dead and All Saints' Day led the Remembrance Day organizers to declare the holiday a general day for the remembrance of the dead. Thus, on November 9th not just those who had died for the Party were to be commemorated, but also those who had died in World War I, in the current war, the victims of aerial bombardment, and indeed dead ancestors in general. The propagandists declared: "On Remembrance Day, 9th of November, it should not only be the custom for each locality to decorate the 'monuments to dead heroes' but the graves of all the other dead as well."[28] By transforming the Remembrance Day for those who fell for the Movement into a general "Day of Remembrance for Ancestors and the Dead,"[29] commemorating the sacrifice of the November 9th martyrs obliged the younger generation to extend their commemoration to all the living and the dead. In this way, and in competition with the Christian belief in the resurrection of the dead and eternal life, the promise of symbolic immortality represented by the Party's martyrs was extended to all Germans: "For us the Eternal Guard in Munich symbolizes this faithful commemoration and at the same time symbolizes eternal life."[30] However, this innovation was a defensive reaction and failed to achieve its purpose.

The myth of November 9th, 1923, did not survive the end of the Third Reich. But before the end an attempt was made to create a new myth based on it, which was hoped would be effective beyond the end of the war. Hitler, the martyr who had "survived" the 1923 sacrifice, should now become the martyr in the new defeat, this time the nation's defeat, and thereby inspire faith in future victory. Goebbels, who understood the business of creating myths as much as his *Fuehrer* did, sketched the plan at a briefing in the

28 *DnG*, 1942, 492.
29 *DnG*, 1944, 353, 357.
30 *DnG*, 1943, 463.

Fuehrer's bunker on April 25th, 1945. "If the *Fuehrer* were to die honorably in Berlin, and Europe become Bolshevik, within five years at the latest, the *Fuehrer* would become a legendary figure and National Socialism a myth made holy by its final great sacrifice."[31]

Hitler took up the idea and sketched the outlines of the new myth in his Political Testament of April 29th: "From the sacrifice of our soldiers and from my solidarity with them unto death, will inevitably spring up in the history of Germany the seed of a radiant renaissance of the National Socialist movement and thus the realization of a true community of the people (*wahre Volksgemeinschaft*)."[32]

The careful wording of the report of Hitler's death that linked it to the "sacrifice of our soldiers" was intended to suggest that Hitler had sought a hero's death in battle. For it was clear that a new myth that promised a rebirth like that of November 9th could only grow out of sacrifice, and not out of the cowardly suicide that Hitler had decided to commit long before April 29th,and which he carried out on April 30th. For this reason Hitler's suicide was kept secret and his death made public in accordance with the new myth. In a radio address on May 1st,Grand Admiral Dönitz, whom Hitler had appointed Reich President, announced Hitler's death: "The German people bow their heads in profound sorrow and respect. Very early he had recognized the horrible danger of Bolshevism and devoted his life to combating it. At the end of this struggle and his life's unwavering path stands his hero's death in the capital of the German Reich. His life was one of selfless devotion to Germany."[33]

Already on the following day the military bulletin found appropriate words for the new myth, especially the ones that presented the Fuehrer's death as a martyr as an obligation for the living: "The Fuehrer has fallen

31 Qouted in: Ralf Georg Reuth, *Goebbels* (Munich: Piper, 1990), 600.

32 "The Private and Political Testaments of Adolf Hitler, April 29, 1945," in Office of United States Chief of Counsel for Prosecution of Axis Criminality, *Nazi Conspiracy and Aggression,* 8 vols. and 2 suppl. vols. (Washington D. C.: Government Printing Office, 1946–1948, VI), 259–263, Doc. No. 3569-PS.

33 *Dokumente der Deutschen Politik und Geschichte von 1848 bis zur Gegenwart*, vol. 5: *Die Zeit der nationalsozialistischen Diktatur 1933–1945*. ed. Johannes Hohlfeld (Berlin: Dokumenten–Verl. Wendler, 1953), 529–530.

at his post at the head of the heroic defenses of the Reich's capital. He gave his life, inspired by the will to rescue his people and Europe from Bolshevist destruction. This exemplary sacrifice, 'faith unto death' is obligatory for all our fighting men."[34]

34 "Wehrmachtsbericht vom 2.5.1945," quoted in Erich Murawski, *Der deutsche Wehrmachtsbericht 1939–1945. Ein Beitrag zur Untersuchung der geistigen Kriegsführung* (Boppard am Rhein: Boldt, 1962), 595.

Take this flag staff in your hands with pride;
Your strength stems from this One flag.

Hans Baumann, "We Ignite the Fire."

CHAPTER 5

CULT

The holiday, "Memorial Day for the Martyrs of the Movement," displayed all the significant formal and material aspects of a cult. It commemorated an event that was deemed to be holy and that was sanctioned by an annual public ritual of renewal. The interpretation of the 9th of November, 1923, as a "salvational event" included the locality, the requisites, and the participating persons: the *Feldherrnhalle* was consecrated as a holy site, the Blood Flag accorded the status of a relic, and both were celebrated as sacred symbols. Those who had taken part in the putsch were hailed as martyrs, and Hitler—the martyr who had eluded death—became the redeemer. Thus the 9th of November was considered to have been a salvic event, the act of revelation whose content was the "millennial realm" ushered in by National Socialism. Of course, it was understood that the millennial realm would last not just for a thousand years, but for eternity. The Eternal Reich[1] in time was conceived to be the end phase of National Socialist sacred history and thus, for National Socialists, the last relevant stage of history. At the 1934 Reich Party Congress Hitler proclaimed: "It is our wish and our intention that this State and this Reich shall live in the coming millennia."[2] In texts that were written for celebrations and commemorations the above named contents and symbols were woven into a myth. The myth made statements about the meaning and purpose of individual and collective existence and in this way held out the promise of salvation, and indeed sought to satisfy the longing for immortality. The cultic celebrations lent an aura of sacred history to the myth.

The fact that the Third Reich developed a veritable cult is a strong argument and sufficient justification for characterizing National Socialism as a political religion. At least at the level of a sociological or phenomenological inquiry, skepticism about applying the concept of religion to a political

1 Herbert Böhme, *Bekenntnisse eines jungen Deutschen* (Munich: Eher, 1935), 28.

2 *Der Kongreß zu Nürnberg vom 5. bis 10. September 1934. Offizieller Bericht über den Verlauf des Reichsparteitages mit sämtlichen Reden* (Munich: Eher, 1934), 213.

ideology—even to an atheistic one—is unfounded. According to Emil Durkheim's classic definition, every religion is made up of a system of "beliefs" and "rites" that are grouped around an organizing center of "sacred objects."[3] And since the National Socialist cult provided ritual affirmations of faith, National Socialism can be regarded as a religion, specifically a political religion.

The National Socialist cult was inspired by Hitler and implemented by Goebbels and others with the intention of making it socially effective. But after 1933 Hitler and the Party leadership journals denied that National Socialist celebrations had anything to do with a cult. As a result, the use of the word "cult" to describe National Socialist celebrations was banned. How can this contradiction be explained?

The torchlight parade on the evening of January 30th, 1933, organized by Goebbels to celebrate the new Chancellor, Adolf Hitler, was the initial act in a series of events and celebrations that took place during the first year of the National Socialist State. With the assumption of power the Movement could now do more than stage party rallies—it was able to organize imposing State pageants. Goebbels declared the day preceding the *Reichstag* election on March 5th, 1933, the "Day of the Awakening Nation" and employed propaganda of every kind to celebrate it throughout the country. The radio broadcast of Hitler's speech in Königsberg, East Prussia, was accompanied by the solemn ringing of bells and an organ playing the Christian hymn, "We Gather Together." March 21st, the "Day of Potsdam" on which the former Field Marshal Hindenburg[4] and the World War One Corporal Hitler joined hands in front of the Garnison Church, marked the first solemn State ceremony under the new rulers' direction. It was followed by May 1st, the day cleverly taken from the socialists by renaming it National Labor Day, later called the National Holiday of the German People. On that day, along with members of the SA, SS, and Hitler Youth, allegedly one million workers gathered in Berlin. Goebbels had a grandstand built on the Tempelhof Field where seventeen thousand spectators witnessed the march of three thousand standard-bearers. The "world's largest public

3 Emile Durkheim, *Die elementaren Formen des religiösen Lebens* (Frankfurt: Suhrkamp, 1981), 61, 67, 70.

4 Paul von Hindenburg, Reichspräsident (President of the Weimar Republic) (1925–1934); General Field Marshal during World War One.

address system" bathed the assembly in sound and the celebration, and all of its speeches were broadcast by radio throughout Germany.[5] For the night ceremony Albert Speer designed the decoration of illuminated flags. It was the journeyman piece that qualified him for the task of outfitting future celebrations and that led to his being commissioned to create the backdrop and structures on the Zeppelin Field in Nuremberg for the Reich Party Congress "Victory" in September.[6] Hitler made the ritual consecration of new flags––a rite that had been observed since 1926––that marked the Congress' liturgical high point. The Party Congress was followed in October by the "Harvest Festival" and on November 9th by the "Memorial Day for the Martyrs of the Movement," an event that first reached its height of ceremonial grandeur in 1935.

Along with celebrations on January 30th and May 1st, the Reich Party Congress, Harvest Festival, and the 9th of November, subsequent years saw the addition of new holidays: Heroes' Memorial Day on March 16th, the *Fuehrer's* Birthday on April 20th, Mothers' Day, the Summer and Winter Solstices, and the HJ and Party induction ceremonies that took place at various times during the year but on no set days. These events constituted the NS calendar of canonical holidays, or "Holidays in the Course of the National Socialist Year." Until the beginning of the war they were generally celebrated elaborately at central *Reich* ceremonies, at smaller venues in *Gau* capitals, and in local Party groups and various Party branches.

In the first years after 1933, the National Socialist celebrations were naively and preferably described as "cultic acts" or "acts of consecration," or the "Thing,"[7] and in other similarly solemn terms. Until 1935 one finds such concepts in the Party's official publications.[8] However, after awhile

5 Eugen Hadamovsky, *Dein Rundfunk. Das Rundfunkbuch für alle Volksgenossen* (Munich: Eher, 1934), 96–99.

6 For the design of the May 1st celebration and the Reich Party Congress, see Albert Speer, *Erinnerungen* (Berlin: Propyläen, 1969), 40–42.

7 A ritual form of outdoor theater that made use of various art forms; in prehistoric times it was the Germanic term for public assemblies and tribunals.

8 Cf. *Vorschläge der Reichspropagandaleitung zur nationalsozialistischen Feiergestaltung* (Munich: Eher, 1935), I/ 6; *Der Parteitag der Freiheit vom 10–16. September 1935. Offizieller Bericht über den Verlauf des Reichsparteitages mit sämtlichen Kongreßreden* (Munich: Eher, 1935), 10.

the excessive use of religious discourse began to displease those in charge of organizing the events. In addition, and apparently under the influence of folkish-religious sectarians that had been absorbed into the NSDAP, "cult activities" were getting out of hand. Patriotic celebrations replete with altars adorned with steel helmets, "brown shirt baptisms," and similar things led to increasingly kitsch laden ceremonies. Goebbels was the first to feel compelled to take steps against these excesses. At a meeting of Propaganda Leaders during the 1935 Reich Party Congress he warned that "it is time to put an end to the work of 'false zealots' who, acting in a vacuum, stage uncalled for ritual acts and fill them with concepts like 'cult' or 'Thing play,' etc., and who, in newspaper articles, go overboard in the use of such terms."[9] In the same year the Ministry of Propaganda and the government's press department issued concrete guidelines governing the use of such language: "To the extent that they are brought into connection with the idea and essence of National Socialism it is high time that the German press dispense with such vague mystical terms as 'Thing,' 'cult,' 'cultic,' etc. It must be made perfectly clear that the Movement will have nothing to do with this kind of mumbo jumbo."[10]

Finally, Hitler intervened to settle the matter once and for all. At the meeting of the Culture Section during the 1938 Reich Party Congress he clarified the relationship between National Socialism and the "cultic": "National Socialism is not a cultic Movement but a *folkish-political doctrine* based exclusively on the knowledge of race. It has no intention of becoming a mystical cult but is committed to leading and fostering the well-being of a people that is resolved to act in accordance with the imperatives of its blood. Therefore we have no cult sites but assembly halls where the people can gather, and we have no places of worship but places to assemble and to parade. We have no cult groves, but sport arenas and playing fields. And our places of assembly are characterized by brightness and light, not by the mystical darkness of cult sites; this is also true for our *functional halls and structures*. Therefore no cultic acts take place in them. They are exclusively dedicated to the kind of folk assemblies that were developed during our

9 Quoted in ibid., 1/20 (October 1935).

10 Quoted in Cornelia Berning, "Die Sprache des Nationalsozialismus," in *ZfDW*, 18., vol. 3 (1962), 166,167 (October 23, 1935).

long years of struggle and with which we are therefore familiar. And we intend to keep it that way."[11]

Hitler's statements were patently false. In the Third Reich there were locations where cult celebrations took place, even if they were also places for assembly and parade. For example, especially the Königsplatz in Munich with its Temples of Honor and the Eternal Guard had a pronounced religious character, and so did the ceremonial sites at the Reich Party Grounds in Nuremberg: The Zeppelin Field's massive staircase crowned by gleaming white colonnades was "without a doubt [...] inspired by the Pergamon Altar," as their architect Speer admitted.[12] In the Luitpold Grove, where the annual roll call of the SA and SS took place, a broad lane extended from the main grandstand to the *Ehrenmal* (war memorial) where Hitler, accompanied at an appropriate distance by the SA Chief of Staff and the *Reichsfuehrer* SS, strode between the mustered formations in a ritual honoring of the dead. Leni Riefenstahl captured this ceremony strikingly in her film of the 1934 Reich Party Congress, "Triumph of the Will." Speer designed the unique platform from which Hitler spoke, the so-called "*Fuehrer*-position," a massive stone plinth that jutted out from the main grandstand. Hitler stood alone on this stone block removed from the others and far above them like an unapproachable high priest on a towering temple wall.

Naturally, the *Feldherrnhalle* in Munich was a place of particular holiness. This was demonstrated not only by the ceremony that took place there each year on "Memorial Day for the Martyrs of the Movement," but also by a daily ritual. And, conversely, its holiness was demonstrated negatively by those who avoided observing the daily ritual. A raised commemorative plaque had been placed on the Residence Street side of the *Feldherrnhalle* and guarded day and night by an "honor guard" made up of two SS men. When a pedestrian walking through the Residence Street to Odeonsplatz passed the plaque he was obliged to salute with raised right arm (the so-called *Hitler-Gruß*) just as a Catholic is expected to bend his knee before the Blessed Sacrament and make the sign of the cross. Those who wished

11 *Der Parteitag Großdeutschland vom 5–12 September 1938. Offizieller Bericht über den Verlauf des Parteitages mit sämtlichen Kongreßreden* (Munich: Eher, 1938), 81. (Italics in the original spaced).

12 Speer, *Erinnerungen,* 68.

to avoid performing the ritual turned off Residence Street shortly before reaching the *Feldherrnhalle* and went through the narrow Viscardi Lane to Odeonsplatz. For this reason Viscardi Lane was known locally as "Shirkers Alley."

It was also false to say that the "mystical darkness of cult sites" did not characterize the spaces and buildings where National Socialist celebrations took place. The fact is that many ceremonies were carried out at night in order to heighten the atmosphere of consecration. This practice began as early as 1933 in Berlin with the First of May evening celebration at the Tempelhof Field. And on Memorial Day for the Martyrs of the Movement it was the custom for the SS-*Verfügungstruppen* (Disposal Troops), the SS-*Totenkopfverbände* (Death's-Head units), and the SS-*Junkerschulen* (Officer Schools) to take their oaths of loyalty at midnight.[13] Likewise, the high point of the annual Reich Party Congress was the evening roll call of the political leaders assembled on the Zeppelin Field. Speer was the lighting director: countless swastika flags that decorated the surrounding walls were illuminated by spotlights; 150 anti-aircraft searchlights created a dome of light over the field. Reports in the Party newspaper, *Völkischer Beobachter*, described the roll call as "a service of worship" and an "hour of consecration, devotion, and prayer."[14]

In view of these facts, why did Hitler deny that National Socialism had anything to do with cults? In a speech to the Reich Party Congress in 1938 he gave this answer: "Our task is not to carry out *cultic acts*, that's the *churches*' business."[15] He rejected the term "cult" because it was already in the hands of the Christian churches and because he wanted to veil the fact that National Socialism did indeed compete with the cult of the Christian

13 *Völkischer Beobachter*, 10.11.1935; *Zum 9. November 1936*, ed. by the NSDAP, Traditionsgau München-Obb. (Munich: Eher, n.d. [1936]); *Vorläufiges Programm für den 8./9. November 1937.* Der Chef der SA-HA. IfZ, MA-386/4993–4999; *Aufmarschstab für den 8./9.11.37 beim Oberabschnitt Süd*. IfZ, MA-386/4977–4984.

14 J. Berchtold, "Die Weihestunde," in *Völkischer Beobachter* , Munich Edition, 12.9.1936, 2; Cf. *Völkischer Beobachter* , Munich Edition, 13.9.1936, 1*VB*, 11.9.1937, 1f.

15 *Der Parteitag Großdeutschland vom 5–12 September 1938,* 82. (Italics in the original spaced).

religion. The use of the concept for National Socialist events was therefore forbidden. At the same time, by rejecting the use of the term for the Party, Hitler tried to discredit the churches and to claim a higher status for his own ideology and the assemblies that celebrated it: "There were ages in which semi-darkness was the prerequisite for the effectiveness of certain doctrines but now we live in an era in which light is the medium of successful action. [...] At the heart of our program we don't find mystical guessing, but the *clarity of knowledge* which is the basis of our *open confession*."[16] With terms like "semi-darkness" and "mystical guessing" Hitler obviously intended to denigrate Christianity and its cult. In contrast, National Socialism's goal was the "clarity of knowledge" and it could therefore be openly professed as the heart of the Party program. It was a clever rhetorical trick: A similar sound and common etymology of the juxtaposed words *Erkennen* (knowledge) and *Bekenntnis* (confession) with a "therefore" inserted in-between, were calculated to give the impression that they belonged together and that the one followed logically from the other. But what is ultimately significant in this connection is that the word *Bekenntnis* (confession of faith)––a word taken from the language of religion—could not be avoided, and was not avoided.

From the very first days of the Third Reich the publications that watched over the organization and structure of National Socialist ceremonies placed the act of confessing faith at their center. Ceremonial programs varied according to their specific purposes and were further differentiated over the years. But they almost always culminated in a confession of faith in the *Fuehrer*, or in some aspect of National Socialist ideology, such as Blood and Soil or *Volk* and *Reich.* For example, at the end of 1935 the Culture Section of the Reich Propaganda Ministry commissioned Herbert Böhme, Herybert Menzel, and Gerhard Schumann to write choral poems for the celebration of Labor Day. All the works––written to the ministry's requirements—had the following structure and parts:

Song celebrating the flag
Fahnenspruch (Sentence that evokes the meaning of the flag.)
Hymn

16 Ibid., 81–82 (Italics in the original spaced).

Invocation
Confession of Faith.[17]

In October 1936 the Association of National Socialist Teachers published the following guidelines for the structure of celebrations in training camps, according to which "the most important elements of a National Socialist confession of faith are:

Invocation
Proclamation
Confession
Such a structure fulfills the requirements for a properly structured ceremony."[18]

In 1940, the Cultural Section of the Reich Youth Leadership issued the following basic plan for the structure of Hitler Youth ceremonies:

1. Thematic Preparation and Introduction (*Fuehrer* quotes)
2. Oration
3. Confession of Faith.[19]

These examples could be easily multiplied.[20]

The purpose of the celebratory programs was to fulfill Hitler's intention of evoking declarations of faith in National Socialism and in his own person. At first, only Party members and members of their organizations were compelled to confess faith by taking oaths, consecrating flags, and committing themselves in formal ceremonies; such acts also

17 Ibid., 1/202, 1/203–205. See Gerhard Schumann, *Feier der Arbeit* (Munich: Langen, n.d.[1936]).

18 *Fest- und Freizeitgestaltung im NSLB. Amtliche Mitteilungsblätter der Hauptstelle Schulung im Hauptamt für Erzieher der NSDAP*. 1. Jg. (1936/37), 10 (Oct. 1936).

19 *Feierstunden und offenes Singen. Material für die Kulturarbeit im Kriege*. Heft 2, ed. Kulturamt der Reichsjugendführung (Berlin n.d. [probably 1940]), 6.

20 Cf. Klaus Vondung, *Magie und Manipulation. Ideologischer Kult und politische Religion des Nationalsozialismus* (Göttingen: Vandenhoeck and Ruprecht 1971), 113–118.

took place in simple holiday camps. However, the ultimate goal was to have the entire people commit itself in this way. At the 1934 Reich Party Congress Hitler proclaimed: "The goal must be that all honorable Germans will be National Socialists! *But only the best National Socialists are Party Comrades*!"[21] Of the latter "more will be required than from the millions of other National Comrades (*Volksgenossen*). It will not be enough for them to declare, 'I believe,' they will pledge, 'I fight!'"[22] According to Hitler, for now, and for the "millions of other National Comrades," the confession "I believe" was enough: But still he demanded this confession of faith from "all honorable Germans" who would one day be National Socialists.[23]

In addition to ceremonies of commitment, party induction ceremonies, and celebrations in vacation camps, the spectacular mass events of the "Holidays in the Course of the National Socialist Year" with their flag consecrations and swearing of oaths were especially effective in bringing about declarations of faith in National Socialism. At large mass events Hitler not only let himself be celebrated as a savior, he also initiated particular rituals and sanctioned others that met with his approval. For example, the organization of the annual Reich Party Congress in Nuremberg was carried out by the "Staff for Organizing Reich Party Congresses." It was directed by Rudolf Schmeer, a co-worker of Robert Ley, who as Reich Organization Leader had overall responsibility for organizing the Party Congress. Other staff members included Hugo Fischer, chief of staff in Goebbels' ministry, and Albert Speer who was responsible for architectural design. Additional departments and sections took responsibility for conducting the various individual events. Before the beginning of a Reich Party Congress Hitler scrutinized the program and made the decisions on particularly important issues. For the rest, the political leaders of the SA, SS, Hitler Youth, and German Labor Front were responsible for their own roll call ceremonies and events. At the end of a Congress Hitler praised or criticized what he had seen, and

21 *Der Kongreß zu Nürnberg vom 5. bis 10. September 1934*, 212 (Italics in the original.)

22 Ibid., 211 (Italics in the original spaced).

23 See above, p. 43.

in this way influenced the organization and structure of the next Congress.[24]

Despite Hitler's rejection of "mystical darkness" he had nothing against nocturnal ceremonies at Party Congresses when they were staged with the sophisticated lighting effects that Speer had designed for the roll call of the political leaders. The cult Hitler promoted was part of a project of instrumental rationality that was entirely modern in its use of propaganda and mass psychology. He took less interest in the structure of Party ceremonies at the level of local groups and branches, and he did not take much interest in other forms of celebration and left their organization to his paladins. Hitler's rejection of the "mystical cult" in 1938 could even be viewed as a criticism of Himmler's and Rosenberg's penchant for mysticism, the longing to create a spiritual order, and the romanticizing of German history and pre-history. In this connection Hitler could not take seriously their creation of ceremonies that involved esoteric rituals.[25] But not only did he decline to interfere with these tendencies, he also tolerated the efforts of other Party leaders to develop similar cult-like ceremonies. As a result the Third Reich offered a broad spectrum of such events.

The Third Reich developed three major types of celebration: "Holidays in the Course of the National Socialist Year," in analogy to the Christian churches' liturgical year; "Life Celebrations," in analogy to baptism, marriage, and funeral ceremonies; and "Morning Celebrations"— consisting of roll calls in the camps of the various branches of the Party, and Sunday "*Weltanschauung* Celebrations"— in analogy to matins and Sunday worship.

Between 1933 and 1939 the "Holidays in the Course of the National Socialist Year" were established with some measure of success, especially at the level of the major "Reich celebrations". With the exception of the Reich Party Congress, where Goebbels had to work with Reich Organization Leader Ley, Albert Speer, and the participating Party organizations, the direction of the Reich celebrations was in his hands. By virtue of his role as Reich Minister for Public Enlightenment and Propaganda, he organized the public holidays and other State ceremonies, and by virtue of

24 Written and oral communications from Albert Speer to the author, February 2nd and March 13th, 1970.

25 See above, chapter two, "Mysticism."

his role as Reich Propaganda Leader he directed the Party celebrations. An order by Hitler on October 20, 1934, confirmed the exclusive right of the Reich Propaganda Directorate to produce the relevant guidelines and directives in these areas.[26] In addition to Reich celebrations, from an early date Goebbels tried to establish such events at the *Gau*, regional, and local level. In April 1935 the Culture section of the Central Party Propaganda Office began to publish the journal, *Suggestions of the Central Party Propaganda Office for Organizing National Socialist Celebrations*. The journal's task was to establish "specific norms" for the structuring of celebrations at lower Party levels and to facilitate their uniform direction.[27] Here, too, the journal's very first issue stressed that the main purpose of National Socialist celebrations is to "inspire the participants" to confess their faith: "It must be our aim to gradually awaken the *desire* in all German citizens to participate again and again in ceremonies that give them the opportunity to confess their faith."[28]

Beginning in 1937, the *Suggestions* appeared under a new name: *The New Community: Party Archive for National Socialist Celebrations and the Structuring of Leisure Activities*. In order to increase its influence on the design and structure of Party celebrations, especially in the Hitler Youth and the SA, Goebbels invited the relevant offices of branch and affiliated associations to join him in an "ongoing cooperation."

After the war began the large Reich celebrations of "Holidays in the Course of the National Socialist Year" were reduced to more modest proportions, or disappeared entirely, while the events in local groups and Party divisions were celebrated in the form of morning or evening ceremonies. During the first year of the war, until victory over France, the interest in National Socialist celebrations faded into the background. But the longer the war went on, and the clearer it became that final victory would not be achieved quickly, the more important ceremonial activities became. It was the ongoing war that made the holding of National Socialist ceremonies all the more important and indeed, in a struggle that was directed not only

26 Karlheinz Schmeer, *Die Regie des öffentlichen Lebens im Dritten Reich* (Munich: Pohl, 1956), 29.

27 *Vorschläge*, 1/16 (1935).

28 Ibid., I/1 (Apr. 1935) (Italics in the original spaced).

against external foes, made them absolutely necessary. In September 1941, and in line with the directives of his superior Goebbels, Karl Cerff, the head of the newly upgraded Main Office of the Cultural Section of the Central Propaganda Office of the NSDAP, wrote in the *New Community*: "It is wrong to think, as some do, that during the war it is inappropriate to hold celebrations; as a matter of fact the contrary is true: at this time the German people are particularly open for the reception of spiritual values. Or do we want to leave this task to other organizations?"[29] This position was emphasized a year later by the head of the Party Chancellery, Martin Bormann (inappropriately enough on Christmas Eve 1942): "Cultural work is especially important now and in the further course of the war it will prove to be one of our most vital and significant instruments. The hearts and minds of our German comrades cry out for support and guidance and we must respond to this need in a sympathetic way."[30]

Since the spectacular Reich celebrations were discontinued during the war, the publications devoted to organizing these celebrations turned increasingly to the smaller and more intimate ones held by local groups and their subdivisions: Life Celebrations and Morning Ceremonies. But Goebbels, who up to this time had been the leading voice in shaping the structure of National Socialist ceremonies, now had competitors. In the Third Reich a notable structural feature of both the State and Party organization was the chaotic appropriation of responsibility. The ensuing fragmentation and overlapping of competencies led to legal uncertainties, rivalries, and to infighting among Party and State offices. Goebbels based his claim to responsibility in this field on the powers accorded to him in the areas of propaganda and culture. His two main rivals, Robert Ley and Alfred Rosenberg, claimed authority to structure celebrations on the basis of their responsibilities in the fields of training and education.

Dr. Robert Ley was not only Reich Organization Leader but also Reich Training Leader. Like Goebbels' Reich Propaganda Directorate, Ley's Main Organization Office and the Main Schooling Office were organized

29 *DnG*, Sept./Oct. 1941, 1.

30 Official announcement B 16/42, December 24th,1942, quoted in *DnG*, May/June 1943, 258.

strictly from the top down. Ley's position as head of the unified labor union, the German Labor Front and the associated NS Community Strength through Joy, afforded him ample opportunity to organize celebrations and leisure activities. He also had influence on the Association of National Socialist Teachers since this organization was part of the NS Community "Strength through Joy." In addition he was chairman of the Staff for organizing the National Socialist Party Congress and the initiator of the National Socialist *Ordensburgen*[31] where the younger generation was trained for Party leadership positions. Thus he had many opportunities to organize festivals and celebrations on his own. However, it was not so much Ley himself but the directors (*Amtsleiter*) under him who were active. As a result the events and their forms were as varied and disparate as was Ley's power sphere in general. The lack of systematic leadership was not due to any disinterest on Ley's part in organizing such ceremonies, but the result of his incompetence. His attempt in 1941 to acquire control of all Party celebrations was defeated by Bormann and thereafter Ley was limited to providing organizational support.[32]

Although Rosenberg had much less power, in the end he was more successful. In 1934 Hitler had appointed him Commissioner for Monitoring the Entire Spiritual and Ideological Education and Training of the NSDAP and Rosenberg staked his claim to responsibility for the structuring of ceremonies on the basis of his competencies in the areas of training and education. But his office lacked the infrastructure necessary to exercise direct influence at lower Party levels. He tried to make up for this deficit through research and planning and in this regard turned his attention first to Life Celebrations.

These were not common in the regime's early years. However, the SS was an exception and Heinrich Himmler diligently planned "marriage consecrations" (*Eheweihen*), later termed more innocuously "wedding ceremonies." He set great store in introducing or reviving customs that he considered to be Germanic. The bride and groom were given bread and salt and two cups. The custom of exchanging wedding rings was continued

31 Training centers in buildings constructed on the model of the Teutonic Knight's castle-fortresses.

32 For details, see Vondung, *Magie und Manipulation*, 51–55, 67–68.

but now the rings symbolized not just that the married couple's love was without beginning or end, but, as Himmler––always pleased to serve as wedding speaker—once put it at the marriage of an SS member, they "also symbolize the wish that your family (*Sippe*) may be a beginning without an end."[33]

Life Celebrations were clearly more in competition with the corresponding Christian baptism, marriage, and funeral rites than were the "Holidays in the Course of the National Socialist Year". And in this regard the introduction of National Socialist Life Celebrations was also part of the fight against the churches. Hitler initially supported the attempt of self-named "German Christians" to create a regime friendly (*gleichgeschaltet*), 'Aryan', Protestant Reich Church; but in reaction to their efforts, the "Confessing Church" was formed and a conflict between the two groups ensued. A controversy between Protestants was not in Hitler's interest and he dropped German Christian Reich Bishop Müller.[34] By decree of the Reich Minister of the Interior, from November 26th, 1936, the concept of "Believers in God" (*Gottgläubige*) was officially introduced to designate "all National Comrades who have turned away from recognized religious communities but who are still believers."[35] In this way people, especially Party members, were given the opportunity to profess a non-Christian religion of whatever kind without having to join a community of faith outside the Party. The Believers in God never became an organized community, and certainly the NSDAP had always intended to remain the sole comprehensive organization in the areas of politics and *Weltanschauung*. For this reason, and particularly for Party members, it seemed only natural to offer substitutes for Christian ceremonies. This was all the more important because not only run of the mill "baptism certificate Christians" who no longer attended church, but also many National Socialist Believers

33 Words spoken by Reichsfuehrer-SS Himmler at the marriage ceremony of SS-Major Deutsch, April 2, 1936. *IfZ*, MA-311/1595–1602. See also Vondung, *Magie und Manipulation*, 98–99.

34 For Hitler's policy toward the churches and their role in the Third Reich (primarily the Protestant Church), see Klaus Scholder, *Die Kirchen und das Dritte Reich*. 3 vols., (Frankfurt: Propylaen, 1977–2001), and Christoph Strohm, *Die Kirchen im Dritten Reich* (Munich: Beck, 2011), especially 35–39.

35 Quoted in *RGG* 3rd ed., vol. 2, col. 109.

in God still adhered loyally to the churches' baptism, wedding, and funeral ceremonies.

The Culture Section of the Reich Propaganda Directorate was the first to turn its attention to wedding ceremonies. Beginning in 1938, it laid down principles and made detailed recommendations on how to combine the civil wedding ceremony with a National Socialist one. Goebbels was not particularly interested in Life Celebrations. In his view they were not spectacular enough, but Rosenberg regarded them as an effective weapon in the struggle against the churches. In a 1941 letter to Bormann he emphasized: "I have devoted my time to this area in particular because Life Ceremonies are the only real tie that millions of National Comrades still have to an organized church toward which they are otherwise completely indifferent."[36] In the following year Rosenberg's office published detailed guidelines for the structure of such ceremonies.[37] The main focus was on wedding ceremonies but recommendations were also made for National Socialist ceremonies concerned with birth and death.

But if Goebbels had left the Life Celebrations to Rosenberg's office without putting up a fight, a bitter conflict arose between the two over the Morning Celebrations. Before the war they had been sporadically held in some training camps of the Association of National Socialist Teachers and in German Labor Service camps, and more often by the HJ. After the creation of the Culture Section of the Reich Youth Leadership guidelines were worked out for Morning services and orders were given to conduct them regularly in HJ camps. A 1937 *Handbook for Cultural Work in Camps* established the celebration's form and structure: Each morning just before breakfast the flag-raising took place. The camp participants gathered around the flag staff, the flag was raised and saluted, the day's watch word issued, and some words of the *Fuehrer* were quoted or a poem was recited. This was followed by a "song hailing the flag" or a "song professing faith." Despite the event's brevity it had an important function. The daily raising of the flag was intended to be a kind of *Weltanschauung* morning prayer to

36 Rosenberg's letter to Bormann July 7, 1941: *IfZ*, MA-545/I251f.

37 *Die Gestaltung der Lebensfeiern. Richtlinien*. ed. Beauftragter des Führers, bearbeitet vom Amt Volkskunde und Feiergestaltung. s. l.[Berlin: Nur für den Dienstgebrauch], 1942.

consecrate the new day and give it direction: "The minute in which the flag is raised and hailed is one of devotion and commitment to the day's tasks."[38] If the daily flag raising ceremony was the equivalent of morning prayer the Sunday Morning Celebration functioned as a substitute for church services. According to the handbook it was intended to "form and strengthen the soul," i.e. to bring about the soul's "'inner mobilization.' [...] It strengthens one's commitment to God, faith in *Fuehrer* and *Volk*, and the will to commit oneself to action."[39] Without a doubt, the proclaimed "commitment to God" was inserted to suggest that the Morning Celebrations were nothing unusual and therefore make it easier for Christian boys and girls to participate. But the decisive passages were those that invoked "faith in *Fuehrer* and *Volk*" and the obligation that followed from this of "committing oneself to action."

The HJ flag raising ceremonies and Morning Celebrations were not affected by the outbreak of the war and the co-operation with Goebbels' Reich Propaganda Directorate was increased. In 1941 when Goebbels returned to the question of organizing ceremonies and celebrations with a renewed and stronger interest he not only upgraded the Culture Section to a Department of Culture (*Hauptkulturamt*) and moved it from Munich to Berlin, but appointed a new and capable director, Karl Cerff, the former director of the HJ's Culture Section. The recruiting of two other senior officials from the HJ also intensified the traditionally close co-operation between the two organizations. Especially the celebrations which affected the Party and the HJ equally—the initiation of the fourteen-year-olds into the HJ and the Party-joining celebration at age eighteen—were conducted jointly. Other Party celebrations that were in Goebbels' area of responsibility were also organized with the help of the HJ.

With the beginning of the war, the above named HJ celebrations and the "Holidays in the Course of the National Socialist Year" were conducted as Morning Celebrations. Goebbels was therefore alarmed when in November 1941 Rosenberg announced that as "an important means of

38 *Freude — Zucht — Glaube. Handbuch für die kulturelle Arbeit im Lager. Im Auftrage der Reichsjugendführung der NSDAP,* ed. Claus Dörner (Potsdam: Voggenreiter, 1937), 37.

39 Ibid., 71, 81.

training" he would be conducting "*Weltanschauung* ceremonies and celebrations for the entire Party and its branches."[40] Rosenberg emphasized "training" as the purpose of these events because this was his area of responsibility and he wanted to keep the celebrations free of influence from Goebbels' Ministry of Propaganda. But if Goebbels had not opposed Rosenberg's claim of responsibility for the Life Ceremonies, he viewed the latter's intention to organize *Weltanschauung* ceremonies in the form of Morning Ceremonies for the entire Party and its branches as an inadmissible interference in his own area of competence. This led to an eighteen month battle between the two leaders and the directors of their respective main offices over who had authority in this area. The argument revolved around the questions of which Morning Celebrations belonged more to the area of propaganda and which served the purpose of training and instruction, and how to distinguish between Party internal celebrations and NSDAP public events. For help in settling the issue the protagonists appealed to the head of the Party Chancellery, Martin Bormann, who over the years had expanded his position into that of an *éminence grise*. Under the pressure of his mediation a compromise was reached in the spring of 1942 and a Party Chancellery directive from May 23, 1942, defined the new tasks: Goebbels retained responsibility for all public events and Reich celebrations during the course of the year and Rosenberg was given control of the Life Ceremonies. For the organization and structure of Morning Ceremonies and similar events the following arrangement went into effect: public ceremonies came under Goebbels' authority, Rosenberg took responsibility for Party internal *Weltanschauung* ceremonies, and Ley was limited to giving organizational support to Goebbels' events and was allowed to "conduct" Rosenberg's. This solution effectively removed Ley from the planning and directing of events. The order also confirmed the practice of close co-operation between the Reich Propaganda Directorate

40 Rosenberg's letter to Goebbels November 26th,1941, *IfZ*, MA-596/389 f.; Rosenberg to Bormann December 29th,1941, *IfZ*, MA-545/1075–1081. Cf. *Weltanschauliche Feierstunden der NSDAP*. Compiled and edited by the *Dienststelle des Beauftragten des Führers für die Überwachung der gesamten geistigen und weltanschaulichen Schulung und Erziehung der NSDAP, Hauptamt Kunstpflege* (Munich: Eher,1944), 7.

and the HJ and emphasized that the HJ was to be "fully" involved in the organization of Party ceremonies.[41]

The conclusion of peace between Goebbels and Rosenberg was the prerequisite for a strong upsurge of activity in the planning of ceremonies and festivals that soon found expression in fundamental changes on the cover of the *New Community*. Beginning in 1942 the journal appeared in a completely new form and the editor was now identified as the "Culture Department of the Reich Propaganda Directorate in Co-operation with the office of *Reichsleiter* Rosenberg (*Dienststelle des Beauftragten des Führers*)." In this way Rosenberg gained an active role in the Party Archive. He had succeeded in enlarging his directorial powers and he was able to exploit them advantageously. Between 1942 and 1944 recommendations and model programs for various kinds of ceremonies appeared in the journal in great number—about forty a year. They were accompanied by an abundance of fundamental articles that clearly demonstrated the nature of the political goals that National Socialism pursued in its celebrations.

As early as May 1942, the month in which Goebbels und Rosenberg settled their differences, a policy article viewed with satisfaction "the growing connection between political, annual, and family ceremonies, the inexorable penetration of the entire range of life's manifestations by the Movement's idea, and thus, the winning-over of the German individual in his entirety for the totality, unity, and exclusiveness of our *Weltanschauung*."[42] The tenor of the article suggests that it was written by Rosenberg or a member of his staff but it in no way contradicted Goebbels's position. Since the ideological aims of Goebbels and Rosenberg were identical their offices quickly learned to work well together. This can be seen clearly in the form that the directives for National Socialist Morning Celebrations took in the same year: "In accord with a principle of the National Socialist *Weltanschauung*, the human body, mind, and soul constitute an indivisible unity; therefore the National Socialist Movement lays unconditional claim to the right *to care comprehensively* for the German people—a care that addresses every National Comrade in his entire being."[43]

41 Der Leiter der Parteikanzlei. *Anordnung A* 25/42 vom 23.5.1942. VOB1. NSDAP 1942, Folge 233.
42 *DnG*, May 1942, H. 5, 213.
43 Ibid., Nov. 1942, H. 11, 595 (Italics in the original spaced).

The claim of the right to care for the entire human being, including the individual's spiritual orientation, again demonstrates National Socialism's attempt to eliminate the distinction between the secular and the religious, which is what made National Socialism a political religion. Here it becomes very clear that National Socialist celebrations were designed to make this claim a reality by bringing the community of celebrants to confess their faith in public: "Thus, along with the rallies designed to inform the people and the enthusiasm-generating demonstrations, the Morning Celebrations should constitute a regularly recurring ceremonious appeal to the depths of the soul (*Seelenkraft*) of every individual member of the Party and people in order that, through regularly repeated declarations of commitment to the community, this firm and deep well of faith will flow over into the national community and, overcoming all apathy, will enable the nation to grow stronger and stronger."[44]

The plans for the further development of National Socialist ceremonies were made in accord with the Party's claim of the right to care for the entire human being. And the longer the war went on the more new kinds of celebration were proposed. In addition to the annually recurring celebrations, Life Celebrations, ceremonies of commitment to the HJ, Party joining ceremonies, Morning Celebrations in the various Party related sections, and the celebrations of the Party's *Weltanschauung*, new festivities were added: school graduation ceremonies and ceremonies for completing an apprenticeship or becoming a master craftsman; celebrations to honor mothers, fallen servicemen, victims of the air war, and men serving in the armed forces; and village community evenings. As late as 1944, and as the crowning effort to encompass the entire human being, Bormann ordered the introduction of National Socialist Family Evenings "as a further means of leadership." The fifth year of war demands that the political leadership "do all it can to bring family life more into the sphere of political work than it has been in the past." The principle must apply "that families, including those with children in the HJ and BDM, be introduced to the National Socialist body of thought together."[45] Towards the end of the Third Reich

44 Ibid.

45 Der Leiter der Parteikanzlei, *Anordnung* 74/44 from April 3rd, 1944; *IfZ*, MA 452/2528–2532.

planning and control measures in the area of structuring festive events reached their high point. According to the ideas of the journals that directed such practice, a fine meshed net of National Socialist celebrations was to be extended over the entire social life of the nation. Indeed the last issue of the *Party Archive for National Socialist Celebrations and the Structuring of Leisure Activities* in January 1945 printed nine proposals for the structuring of National Socialist celebrations. The intentions of the Party offices and their directors, Goebbels, Rosenberg, and Bormann were clearly recognizable, and in no way contradicted those of Hitler, Himmler, and other leading National Socialists. After the war was won the National Socialist ideology was to be established as a political religion, and as a cult that would permeate every aspect of life with the claim to total and exclusive validity.

But what was the reality of the matter? Were the measures taken to establish a National Socialist cult successful? During the pre-war years the large scale celebrations had been well received. The hundreds of thousands of people who Goebbels was able to mobilize to celebrate May 1st, Harvest Festival, and the 9th of November, or who came of their own free will, were for the most part deeply impressed by the ceremonies' elaborate and sophisticated organization and staging. This is also true for the Reich Party Congresses. Unprejudiced foreign diplomats like the French Ambassador Francois-Poncet described vividly the "atmosphere of universal enthusiasm," the "extraordinary enthusiasm that seized hundreds of thousands of men, the romantic excitement and mystical ecstasy to which they succumbed—a kind of holy madness."[46] Leni Riefenstahl's film of the 1934 Reich Party Congress shows a euphoria among the people which was not staged, and which was also documented in the weekly newsreels that reported on Party Congresses and other festive occasions. Moreover, the Reich Propaganda Direction permitted the documentation of many celebrations in film. For example, already in 1934 a color film was made of the 1934 Harvest Festival at Mount Bückeberg near Hameln. A second film of the 1935 Harvest Festival shows Hitler mounting a slope along an elevated path to the Harvest Altar, flanked on both sides by a crowd of peasants estimated to number one million people. An official press guideline from

46 Quoted in Hermann Glaser, *Das Dritte Reich. Anspruch und Wirklichkeit* (Freiburg: Herder, 4th ed., 1963), 72.

1937 reads: "It is the *Fuehrer's* wish that in the future the Bückeberg's central path, which the *Fuehrer* takes each year on his way to the demonstration, will be called 'The Path Through the People.' The use of any other name is forbidden."[47] And the 1935 film shows the ecstatic homage that the peasants who lined both sides of the path paid the *Fuehrer* as he made his way to the summit.[48]

The major celebrations with their impressive spectacle and solemn ritual generated an emotional excitement that could well be experienced as the form of salvation that Hanns Johst had longed for in 1928, which offering "relief and redemption" from the "distorted reality of the day" brought salvation to the community of those who share "the same ethos, the same will, and the same faith."[49] The major Reich Celebrations were broadcast by all German radio stations and through the practice of "community reception" often constituted the heart of local celebrations. In this way radio broadcasts multiplied the effects of the cultic events.

Some of the HJ celebrations made an especially strong impression, especially those that had been designed artistically or which took place on particularly hallowed ground, such as the consecration of the *Jungvolk* flags (at the supra-regional organizational level, the *Jungbann*) in the Great Refectory of the Marienburg on the 24th of January, 1935, the anniversary of the death of Herbert Norkus. The Hitler Youth member Norkus, who had been murdered by communists in 1932, was a martyr for the HJ as Horst Wessel was for the SA.[50] At the flag consecrating ceremony Eberhard Wolfgang Möller's choral poem, "The Commitment," was performed accompanied by the music of Georg Blumensaat. The Reich Radio station in Königsberg broadcast the ceremony to stations throughout the country.[51] For major celebrations Goebbels used modern media, film and radio, in

47 Quoted in Schmeer, *Die Regie des öffentlichen Lebens im Dritten Reich*, 162.

48 *"Bückeberg"— Feier des nationalsozialistischen Erntedankfestes October 6, 1935*. Filmedition G 187. Author of the publication: Klaus Vondung. Edited by the *Institut für den Wissenschaftlichen Film*, Göttingen 1984.

49 Hanns Johst, *Ich glaube! Bekenntnisse* (Munich: Langen, 1928), 75.

50 In the same year Karl Aloys Schenzinger treated the fate of this member of the Hitler Youth in the novel *Der Hitlerjunge Quex*, which was made into a film the following year.

51 See above, p. 37.

order to reach the largest possible audience. Until the war broke out HJ Morning Celebrations of artistic quality with choral poetry and musical accompaniment were broadcast at irregular intervals, usually on Sunday mornings.[52] Such broadcasts and those of the large National Socialist celebrations made radio an important instrument in the new National Socialist cult. In 1934 German (*Reich*) Radio Programming Director Eugen Hadamovsky stated: "What the church building is for religion, radio will be for the cult of the new State."[53] The Hitler Youth, other branches of the NSDAP, and the Party's smallest local units joined in the practice of the "community reception" of National Socialist celebrations. Also, the rituals of the more modest Morning Celebrations and flag-raising ceremonies in HJ camps did not fail to have an effect on receptive adolescents.

However, during the war the resonance for National Socialist celebrations decreased noticeably. The large Reich Celebrations could no longer be held and the *Fuehrer*, the central figure of cultic veneration, had withdrawn to his headquarters and was no longer a visible presence. From about 1942 onward, the planning and designing of ceremonial programs increased continually and reached its peak just before the end of the Third Reich. But day to day practice lagged behind theory. Although, apart from a few statistics from smaller regions that cover a limited time and which survived more or less by accident, there are no records of how many National Socialist celebrations were actually held during the war,[54] there is important information on this subject in the "Reports From the Reich"—and beginning in the summer of 1943, "SD-Reports on Domestic Issues"—that were regularly compiled by the SS-Security Service from agents throughout the country. Prepared for the highest Party officials with the intention of giving an unvarnished picture of the people's mood and reaction to various events,[55] they also reported regularly on a variety of National Socialist celebrations.

52 See Vondung, *Magie und Manipulation*, 89.

53 Quoted by Claudia Schmölders, "Die Stimme des Bösen. Zur Klanggestalt des Dritten Reiches," in *Merkur. Deutsche Zeitschrift für europäisches Denken* 51 (1997), 683.

54 See Vondung, *Magie und Manipulation*, 108.

55 On the SD-Reports see the detailed information provided by the Introduction to the documents edited by Heinz Boberach, *Meldungen aus dem Reich 1938–*

The record shows that during the war their number declined steadily. Often there were simply not enough trained people available to conduct them in a professional manner. The report at the end of 1943, that "in number and quality" the Harvest Festivals in both the urban and rural areas "had suffered a major decline,"[56] was also true for other kinds of ceremonies. Most of all, support had diminished for ceremonies in addition to the Harvest Festivals and the Life Celebrations that competed with church celebrations. The 1943 SD-Report noted: "According to almost identically worded reports from all regions of the Reich the Party Harvest Festivals were greatly overshadowed and sometimes almost entirely eclipsed by the churches' Harvest Thanksgiving." The statement of one peasant was typical: "We give thanks to the Lord not to the Party."[57]

For awhile a new kind of ceremony that had come into existence due to the war enjoyed a measure of acceptance. On August 8th, 1940, Goebbels established the ceremony of honoring those killed in action, the so-called *Heldenehrungsfeiern* (Ceremonies to Honor Heroes). The ceremony cleverly dispensed with overt propaganda. The relatives of the fallen were invited personally, picked up and accompanied by members of the HJ and BDM, and greeted, as well as discharged, by the representative of the public authority. The ceremony was to be held in a bright and cheerful room, be simple and unadorned, and the eulogy was to be kept personal. The ceremony even dispensed with the *Sieg Heil* to the *Fuehrer* and Greater Germany that generally concluded a celebration. The SD-Reports noted that "when carried out with appropriate solemnity" the NSDAP's ceremonies honoring those killed in action[58] "are generally received thankfully by the mourners and by the public."[59] But as the war continued and the number

1945). Die geheimen Lageberichte des Sicherheitsdienstes der SS. 17 vols. (Herrsching: Pawlak, 1984), vol. 1, 11–44.

56 SD-B, 15.11.1943; Boberach, ed., *Meldungen aus dem Reich*, vol. 15, 6007. In the preceding year there had also been some positive reports; cf. MadR, 7.12.1942; Boberach ed., *Meldungen aus dem Reich*, vol. 12, 4538–4546.

57 SD-B, 15.11.1943; Boberach, ed., *Meldungen aus dem Reich*, vol. 15, 6012–6013.

58 This designation was used since 1943.

59 *MadR*, 15.6.1942; Boberach ed., *Meldungen aus dem Reich*, vol. 10, 3830; cf. *MadR*, 12.10.1942; ibid., vol. 11, 4311–4316. See also *DnG*, 1942, 574, 599 f.; 1943, 437, 499 and *Die Heldenehrungsfeiern der NSDAP*, edited by the *Reichs-*

of casualties and air raid victims mounted acceptance declined. With the ubiquity of death grew the desire for salvation in the Christian sense. And the SD-Reports that complained of the waning success of these ceremonies pointed out that the pastor had it easier because he could offer consolation with a view toward the hereafter, while the public representative "had to appeal to National Socialist values" and, "above all, had to emphasize the fact that the soldier who had been killed in action had fallen for the Reich and that his family should be proud of this fact."[60]

As with the ceremony honoring those killed in action, for a time those celebrating motherhood, and the artistically structured *Weltanschauung* celebrations, were well received because they dispensed with outright propaganda. Likewise, the celebrations of the HJ were well received, even the simply organized roll call and induction ceremonies during the war. The HJ celebrations skillfully exploited the willingness of young people to serve and to make sacrifice. They combined the cult of youth with the romance of adventure and a solemn atmosphere with various ceremonies of commitment, and often joined these elements together with stirring songs. Perhaps the most famous of these is "Forward! Forward! Blare the Bright Fanfares" (*Vorwärts! Vorwärts! Schmettern die hellen Fanfaren*), text by Baldur von Schirach and melody by Hans Otto Borgmann. It was first introduced in the 1933 film *Hitler-Youth Quex*. The text reads in part:

Youth! Youth!
We are soldiers of the future.
Youth! Youth!
In us live the coming deeds.
Fuehrer, we belong to you,
We comrades, belong to you!

Then the refrain:

propagandaleitung der NSDAP, Hauptamt Kultur. Printed in manuscript, extended re-print from "Die neue Gemeinschaft." Nur für Parteidienststellen, n.d. (Berlin c. 1941), 61 et. passim.

60 *MadR*, 12.10.1942; Boberach, ed., *Meldungen aus dem Reich*, vol. 11, 4313; SD-B, 9.8.1943. Cf. ibid., vol. 14, 5583–5590.

The waving flag precedes us,
Our flag is the new day.
And the flag leads into eternity!
Yes the flag triumphs over death![61]

Songs like this and the celebration of youthful martyrs, for example the HJ member Herbert Norkus, alias Quex, inculcated young people with the spirit of self-sacrifice. In his closing speech at the Reich Party Congress in 1934 Hitler declared: "But even if the older among us should falter, the young people are committed to us body and soul!"[62] In this judgment Hitler was not entirely wrong. Indeed, in a certain sense, his words prophesied what was to come. For even in the last days of the war the Hitler Youth was still willing to act as anti-aircraft battery helpers, serve as child soldiers, and to sacrifice their lives for the *Fuehrer*––conduct that, in some measure, was the result of the cult-enhanced ceremonies in which they had participated.

61 Quoted from *Wir Mädel singen. Liederbuch des Bundes Deutscher Mädel*. Edited by the *Reichsjugendführung* (Wolfenbüttel and Berlin: Kallmeyer 2nd expanded ed, 1938), 96–97.

62 *Der Kongreß zu Nürnberg vom 5. bis 10. September 1934*, 214.

The shaping powers of race and landscape, the flow of the ages, and the fructifying harvest of the sheaves of folk culture would not have become a living reality without the scholar's discerning eye.

Professor Dr. Herbert Cysarz, *Das Deutsche Schicksal im Deutschen Schrifttum.*

CHAPTER 6

THEOLOGY

The texts that were read or performed in the National Socialist cult—poems and songs, quotations from the *Fuehrer's* speeches and *Mein Kampf*—articulated faith in the National Socialist world view and led to further confessions of faith. The literary scholar Erich Trunz[1] coined the term *Weihedichtung* (consecration poetry) for the literary texts that were used in National Socialist liturgical celebrations. According to Trunz, "consecration poetry" which is attuned to the "psychic attitude of the celebration" and "borne by emotion and faith" has the task of "interpreting the meaning of our path and of watching over its great principles."[2] But for other literary scholars, even for some who thought in the same ideological categories—for example the influential Hellmuth Langenbucher[3]—it was not merely consecration poetry in the strict sense of the term that interpreted and gave meaning to life, but all "folkish" and "species-appropriate" (*artgemäß*) contemporary literature, i.e. all National Socialist literature that exalted Blood and Soil, *Volk*, *Reich*, and *Fuehrer.*[4] According to Erich Trunz the noblest task of true German literature is "the search for meaning."[5] According to Herbert Cysarz, this meaning is "a most inward meaning,"[6] or indeed, in Heinz

1 1935 assistant, 1938 lecturer at the University of Freiburg; 1940 Professor for Modern German Literature at the German University in Prague.

2 Erich Trunz, "Tatsachendichtung und Weihedichtung," in *Zeitschrift für deutsche Bildung* 11 (1935), 545.

3 Hellmuth Langenbucher was a leading National Socialist historian of literature, writer, and Party functionary.

4 Hellmuth Langenbucher, *Nationalsozialistische Dichtung. Einführung und Übersicht* (Berlin: Junker und Dünnhaupt, 1935), 15.

5 Erich Trunz, *Deutsche Dichtung der Gegenwart. Eine Bildnisreihe* (Berlin: Stilke, 1937), 13.

6 Herbert Cysarz, *Das Deutsche Schicksal im Deutschen Schrifttum. Ein Jahrtausend Geisteskampf um Volk und Reich* (Leipzig: Reclam, 1942), 58. Herbert Cysarz was Professor of Modern German Literature at the German University in Prague.

Kindermann's[7] superlative, the "most intimate meaning."[8] Where the struggle for meaning succeeds—what Trunz expected of true German literature—it "gives meaning" to life, possibly even revealing the "meaning of last things."[9] The "giving of meaning" addresses the soul directly and the poet's calling is to give "form to the spiritual,"[10] a task that in Trunz's view was performed particularly well by the consecration poetry of the National Socialist cult.

This is not the usual language of literary criticism, not even of literary studies in the 1920s and early 1930s. As a matter of fact, the language of interpretation in the texts I have quoted (and many more could be cited) does not use genuine concepts of literary criticism at all but a discourse that is obviously religious. Clearly its purpose is to lend a religious quality to *artgemäße deutsche Dichtung*, above all to consecration poetry, but also to other forms of National Socialist literature. In this regard the texts of literary scholars are unambiguous. A few examples will suffice: Walther Linden[11] saw in Dietrich Eckart's work "a new religious attitude," found "devout religious feeling" in Heinrich Anacker's poems, and noted that in a poem by Baldur von Schirach "with an almost excessive power, the political sphere is re-interpreted religiously."[12] Herbert Böhme, Gerhard Schumann, and other young National Socialist writers were characterized by their "religious drive," "religious feeling for the cosmos," "religious conviction," and above all by their "deep and intimate blending of the religious with the folkish."[13] Erich Trunz asserted that the proletarian poets who had converted to National Social-

7 Heinz Kindermann became a professor for the History of German Literature and German Theater at the University of Münster in 1936, and at the University of Vienna in 1943.

8 Heinz Kindermann, *Kampf um die deutsche Lebensform. Reden und Aufsätze über die Dichtung im Aufbau der Nation* (Vienna: Wiener Verlag, 1944), 16.

9 Trunz, *Deutsche Dichtung der Gegenwart*, 8–9.

10 Ibid., 37, 64.

11 Literary historian and director of the scholarly section of the journal *Zeitschrift für Deutschkunde*.

12 Walther Linden, "Die völkische Lyrik unserer Zeit," in *Zeitschrift für Deutschkunde* 49 (1935), 452.

13 Ibid., 453f., 456–457.

ism brought a "new religious inspiration" to literature.[14] Heinz Kindermann postulated that the foundation of true German literature had to be "folkish religiousness."[15] For Arno Mulot[16] literature dedicated to National Socialist ideas of faith had proved to be a "revelation" that "creates a new community" and "brings about the eternal folk."[17] And in his speech at the burning of books in Bonn on May 10th, 1933, Hans Naumann[18] demanded: "We want a body of literary work in which family and home (*Heimat*), folk and blood, and, in short, the entire life of pious ties is again sacred."[19]

The last quotation demonstrates clearly the function of this religious discourse. It took literature out of the mundane sphere and elevated it to the level of the sacred. And because its contents had been pronounced "holy"—family, home, folk, blood, and other elements—literature itself became sanctified. Naturally, what is sacred is in the highest sense true, inviolable, and binding. Thus the impression was given that literature embodies existential meaning and that one must have faith in it and live one's life according to it.

When literary works are treated as sacred texts it is only natural that authors take on the aura of holy men. Indeed Hellmuth Langenbucher raised poets to the status of "prophets and augurers,"[20] Erich Trunz to "givers of meaning," "spiritual guides," and "law givers,"[21] and Heinz Kindermann to "visionaries and prophets" who perform the task of a "priestly office."[22] Hans Naumann called for a "poet [...] to educate us, to judge us,

14 Trunz, *Deutsche Dichtung der Gegenwart*, 45.

15 Heinz Kindermann, "Junge Dichtergeneration in Front. Ein Bericht," in *Völkische Kultur* 3 (1935), 35.

16 Lecturer, in 1939 Professor for the History of German Literature at the *Hochschule für Lehrerbildung* (Pedagogical Institute) in Düsseldorf.

17 Arno Mulot, *Die deutsche Dichtung unserer Zeit* (Stuttgart: Metzler 2nd ed., 1944), 574.

18 Professor for Early German Literature at the University of Bonn.

19 Hans Naumann, *Kampf wider den undeutschen Geist* (Bonn: Gebr. Scheuer, 1933), 5.

20 Langenbucher, *Nationalsozialistische Dichtung*, 15.

21 Trunz, *Deutsche Dichtung der Gegenwart*, 54.

22 Heinz Kindermann, ed., *Des deutschen Dichters Sendung in der Gegenwart* (Leipzig: Reclam, 1933), 9.

and to give us laws, for the poet's high calling makes him a messenger of god."[23]

Since the works of *arteigene volkhafte Dichtung* were sacred texts communicating revelations, and since the authors were visionaries, prophets, and priests, the discipline concerned with these authors and texts occupied a place high above other disciplines. The "new science of literature," remarked Heinz Kindermann, would no longer be mere philology but a "folkish science of life." It will achieve this end "when, what we used to call service in support of the folk's life-interests and the will to self-assertion, develops indirectly into the occasion for action, and most of all when it becomes the source of courage and valor."[24] In relationship to the religious poetry that imparted meaning to life, the "folkish science of life" went far beyond the interpretation of texts to take on a role much like theology.

In what follows, when we speak of theology we do not mean what Carl Schmitt understood by the term "political theology," to which he gave a specific meaning. What we here call National Socialist "theology" went far beyond Schmitt's definition. In his *Political Theology*, published in 1922, Schmitt introduced his definition of the concept with the now famous sentence: "All significant concepts of the modern theory of the State are secularized theological concepts."[25] With the example of the concept of sovereignty, Schmitt then explained that in the seventeenth century theory of the State the position of the monarch was "exactly analogous to that attributed to God in the Cartesian system of the world." Schmitt also found a corresponding "politization of theological concepts" in Rousseau.[26]

National Socialist "theology" referred to something quite different. The meaning of the "political religion" of National Socialism was the doctrine of National Socialist objects of faith, expressed as faith in Blood and Soil, *Volk* and *Reich*, and in the *Fuehrer* as the representative of these objects. This is not the notion of Hitler as a sovereign being who is analogous to

23 Naumann, *Kampf wider den undeutschen Geist*, 6.

24 Heinz Kindermann, *Dichtung und Volkheit. Grundzüge einer neuen Literaturwissenschaft* (Berlin: Junker und Dünnhaupt, 1937), 49.

25 Carl Schmitt, *Political Theology. Four Chapters on the Concept of Sovereignty*. Translated by George Schwab (Cambridge, MA: MIT Press, 1985), 38.

26 Ibid., 46.

God due to his unlimited power to rule, rather in the faith of National Socialists, the *Fuehrer is* the savior. Herbert Böhme wrote: "You stride among the people as its redeemer."[27] What is expressed here is not a secularization of theological concepts but a theological interpretation of the National Socialist ideas of faith. What form did this interpretation take?

In order to clarify the structure and function of the National Socialist theology of literature and to further differentiate the meaning of its contents, I will compare it to Christian theology. Two preliminary notes: First, obviously the content of the religious discourse conducted by literary scholars in the Third Reich differs widely from that of Christian theology. The basis for comparing the two is their use of language in which similarities become obvious. These enable us to recognize the language of National Socialism as a form of religious discourse. Naturally the comparison between the National Socialist theology of literature and Christian theology is not intended to demean the latter. I compare structures and functions that are characteristic of theological discourse but it is not my intention to draw parallels with regard to content and values. Second, when one considers just how elaborate and complex the systems of Christian theology are, there is no reason to expect that a comparison will yield results in detail. However in certain fundamental areas there are striking similarities.

Experience (*Erfahrungen* and *Erlebnisse*) is the most intimate sphere and the inviolable center of religious discourse. In religious discourse what is understood as divine or godly manifests itself directly without intellectual speculation; the experience takes place in the soul, not in the mind. It is accompanied by such feelings or stirrings of the soul as veneration, fear, devotion, longing, and love. Religious experience is the firmest foundation of faith. Theology interprets, evaluates, and classifies such experiences and their modes of articulation. The National Socialist theology of literature does something very much like this. First, it declares experience (*das Erlebnis* or *Erleben*) to be the essential and indispensible basis of *volkhafte Dichtung*. Literature that had this foundation earned the highest praise, for example when Erich Trunz wrote of a text: "There is not a sentence in it that is not based on experience."[28] Experience was so highly valued because

27 Herbert Böhme, *Das deutsche Gebet* (Munich: Eher, 1936), 14.

28 Trunz, *Deutsche Dichtung der Gegenwart*, 49.

it actually contains a religious quality: it is the indubitable foundation of faith. "The poets themselves are believers."[29] The contents of experience in which the writers believed and then reproduced in literature, and in which the reader was also expected to believe, are what we generally refer to as the elements of National Socialist ideology. But for the National Socialist theology of literature they constituted a religious doctrine. For example, Walther Linden interpreted Gerhard Schumann's poems that celebrate the *Fuehrer* and *Reich* as expressions of "a most profound experience" and the result of a "religious emotion": "It is precisely these poems that point to the continuing, living, and fruitful development of a poet in whom the truly fateful questions of *Reich* and *Volk* are at the heart of his deepest experiences and who approaches these questions from an all encompassing religious feeling for the world."[30]

Like Christian theology, National Socialist theology also developed the typical symbols that crystallize around religious experience: "feeling" and "faith" (Trunz),[31] "vision" and "intuition," and a further "intuitive vision" (Linden),[32] as well as "depth" and "soul" (Trunz).[33] The highest form of religious experience is divine revelation. Although in Christian doctrine it is God who acts, for God reveals Himself, revelation has a human side as well since God reveals himself to human beings. This mutual relationship is also present in the National Socialist theology of literature. The symbol of "revelation" (Mulot)[34] was used to designate the poet as a person who had received a sacred vision and proclaimed its contents holy, for example, the "spirit of the people" (Trunz)[35] and the "Folk-Community" (Mulot).[36]

In general, our knowledge of religious experience, and particularly of the experience of revelation, is gained through texts. Such texts are the objects of the first part of Christian theology, Biblical theology, which inter-

29 Ibid., 53.

30 Linden, "Die völkische Lyrik unserer Zeit," 456.

31 See above footnote 2.

32 Walther Linden, "Volkhafte Dichtung von Weltkrieg und Nachkriegszeit," in *Zeitschrift für Deutschkunde* 48 (1934), 3.

33 See above footnotes 10 and 21.

34 See above footnote 17.

35 Trunz, *Deutsche Dichtung der Gegenwart*, 25. Cf. 9.

36 Mulot, *Die deutsche Dichtung unserer Zeit*, 574.

prets the Old and New Testaments through hermeneutics as its most important method. These interpretations are examined and evaluated in a second part of Christian theology, systematic theology. The results of systematic theology, primarily in the subsections dogmatics and ethics, constitute the basis of a third part, practical theology.[37] The National Socialist theology of literature shares many structural similarities with this model.

It was the Third Reich's religious discourse that made its literary scholars' method of interpretation appear to be more of a theological hermeneutic than a literary one. Texts were treated like sacred writings and said to convey definitive meanings for the conduct of life––they were "orientation in ultimate things."[38] As in systematic theology, the meaning of the text was subdivided into the truths of faith and moral laws. For example, Erich Trunz begins his book *Contemporary German Literature* with a hermeneutics of "experience" that he takes from novels that deal with World War I, and in his analysis comes to the conclusion that "community" is the truth of faith that is revealed in such experience. In the literature that deals with the peasant (*Bauerntum*) he found the "faith in Blood and Soil."[39] Other literary scholars also emphasized these supreme dogmas, often prefacing them with the syllable "new" to deepen their eschatological aura. This took place primarily in the context of the "sacred history" in which Hitler's seizure of power was interpreted as a resurrection. In this regard Heinz Kindermann declared that the "re-birth" of 1933 was the prerequisite for bringing forth the "new German human being."[40] Likewise, Arno Mulot saw the old German society transformed into a "new community."[41] In addition to the dogmas of Blood and Soil, of the new human, and of the transformed folk-community (*Volksgemeinschaft*), there was also the truth of faith that the *Fuehrer* is the messiah. Literary scholarship reinforced the sacral transformation of the *Fuehrer* into the savior that is found in many National Socialist literary works. For example, Walther Linden dogmatized the acts of Hitler that authors had experienced and recorded as acts of salvation:

37 This of course is a simplified outline of Christian theology.

38 Trunz, *Deutsche Dichtung der Gegenwart*, 8.

39 Ibid., 5–9, 30.

40 Kindermann, *Des deutschen Dichters Sendung in der Gegenwart*, 265.

41 Mulot, *Die deutsche Dichtung unserer Zeit,* 574.

"If in Schirach the redemption through the *Fuehrer* is presented as an experience that penetrates to the depths of the soul [...] in Menzel it takes the form of a profound religious stirring."[42]

That the theological hermeneutics of literature also led to the formulation of moral law, is clearly indicated by the practice of calling poets "law givers" (Trunz, Naumann).[43] The framework of these moral laws was described generally, and rather vaguely, as a "new attitude" that emerges from experiences of a religious nature. Thus Walther Linden spoke of the "transformation of the soul that seeks a new moral and religious attitude."[44] For Erich Trunz the "new attitude" came primarily from the experiences of those who had fought at the front in World War I. Codified in literary works this attitude provided the model for a "new life." "The task was to prevent this tremendous and overwhelming experience from being forgotten. For its final meaning had just now become clear: To make this spiritual heritage fruitful, and from the new attitude to create a new life. For the soldiers of the world war the attitude was a living reality, it had no foundation in reason and had not been fashioned by laws of thought; it was simply present as life and could only be passed on to others as life: an exemplary life, lived in the past, alive now in community, and to be re-lived in the future. And yet, there was also another way it could be passed on––it could be given form in literature. In this way literature became the preserver of experiences and an inexhaustible fountain of strength that flowed directly into all aspects of the people's life. To literature fell the immense task of preserving the eternal models of life in human figures and types, and in their fates."[45]

Heroism was the supreme virtue of the new attitude and the ideal and model to be imitated: "The hero suffers and dies as no other because it is his duty to do so."[46] Heroism should be realized in all life situations. Beyond this, other virtues of the "attitude" were often related to heroism. Heinz Kindermann listed the most important ones: "[T]he individual's

42 Linden, "Die völkische Lyrik unserer Zeit," 453.
43 See above footnotes 21 and 23.
44 Linden, "Die völkische Lyrik unserer Zeit," 453.
45 Trunz, *Deutsche Dichtung der Gegenwart*, 8.
46 Ibid., 10.

integration into the organic community (*Organik und Einordnung*), self-discipline and veneration, the combative spirit, the affirmation of community, loyalty to the people and trust in the *Fuehrer*, the willingness to sacrifice, and faith in God."[47]

The exposition of ethics marks the transition to practical theology. Its sphere of action is the religious community. It is therefore logically consistent that National Socialist theology interpreted the "folk-community" as an "intimate (*innere*) community of faith."[48] To the extent that literary scholarship had taken on the role of practical theology it had to develop a new conception of itself. Thus Heinz Kindermann declared that he viewed "literary science as a folkish science of life,"[49] i.e. as a practical science with a direct influence on society. But, in the sense in which National Socialism understood the term, it was not just literary science that assumed the tasks of practical theology. Eugen Hadamosky, by the grace of Goebbels Director of German Radio, attributed this function to radio broadcasting. In his eyes the "Third Reich [...] is not a State structure but a community of faith dedicated to the missionary struggle of National Socialism."[50]

The most important task of the "folkish science of life" was to demonstrate how literature leads from religious experience, through the revelation of National Socialist faith, to action. Arno Mulot wrote: "The German poet has come home to his people. What he received through the grace of this encounter he gives back in the form of the German folkish vision of the world and god. And the people recognizes itself in his poetry. Literature becomes a life-force (*Lebensmacht*) and its language, born of the community, creates a new community. The circle closes: out of the encounter comes revelation, out of revelation proceeds the call, and from the call comes the deed. Folkish literature, dedicated to the folkish rebirth of the people, brings about the eternal folk."[51]

47 Kindermann, *Des deutschen Dichters Sendung in der Gegenwart*, 266.

48 Rudolf Bach, "Das Wesen des Sprech- und Bewegungschores," in *Völkische Kultur* 2 (1934), 213.

49 See above footnote 24.

50 Eugen Hadamovsky, *Der Rundfunk im Dienste der Volksführung* (Leipzig: Noske, 1934), 13.

51 Mulot, *Die deutsche Dichtung unserer Zeit*, 574.

At the center of religious praxis we find the confession of faith. The creed joins individuals together; its function is to radiate into everyday life and to harmonize the people's attitudes and acts with the creed's implicit moral laws and dogmas. The National Socialist theology that became practical theology instilled the reader with the conviction that he must commit himself to the faith and virtues professed by folkish literature, for example the virtue of heroism. As Erich Trunz wrote: "It is not the poet's intention to praise the hero. His work of veneration consists in presenting an artistic *Gestalt* that is so faithful to the original that the reader will feel compelled to commit himself to it."[52]

But not even this was enough. Beyond presenting folkish literature as sacred texts that required the reader to commit himself to, and act on, the virtues they annunciated, the National Socialist "theologians" confessed their own faith and formulated interpretations of literature in the language of confession. For example, Hellmuth Langenbucher gave the preface to his *National Socialist Literature* the title "Confession" (*Bekenntnis*) and used it to profess his faith in what he believed National Socialist literature embodied: "We speak of National Socialist literature and by that we mean a faith in what is coming because it must come."[53]

A particularly impressive confession of faith was given by Hans Naumann at the burning of books in 1933. Naumann, a scholar of high standing and good taste, and an admirer of Thomas Mann, conducted a veritable conversion in public. He began with a confession of sins and called upon the students to burn "what could seduce and endanger you and all of us. [...] This fire is a symbol and it should be a call to us to purify our hearts as well. We are all very much in need of that, all of us without exception; therefore let us also pass judgment on ourselves."[54] The purgation of the heart leads to the rejection of evil, to turning away from the "poison" of the "Un-German spirit," and finally to the new confession of faith: "'To be heroic', they used to say, 'was of no interest to the left,' nor was it sacred to the left, but the left's days are over, and now it is again 'something of inter-

52 Trunz, *Deutsche Dichtung der Gegenwart*, 11.
53 Langenbucher, *Nationalsozialistische Dichtung*, 7.
54 Naumann, *Kampf wider den undeutschen Geist*, 3–4.

est,' and not just 'something of interest' but much more than that, an imperative, a commanding faith, and an ardent prayer."[55]

This religious discourse was directed toward practice. The meaning that it imparted was intended to organize social behavior and action. As a "science of life," literary science sought to influence social life and in this way assumed the character of practical theology. It interpreted, dogmatized, and proclaimed the meaning that was found in literature and which was attributed to literature. Naturally, writers in the roles of prophets and visionaries were of even greater practical importance to a society understood as a community of faith. For through their works they influenced attitudes and action directly, especially through the literary genre that Erich Trunz called "consecration poetry." The staging of consecration poetry in the National Socialist cult was the practical realization of what literature theology had formulated as dogmatics and ethics. In the strictest sense of *kerygma*, consecration poetry was the annunciation and the occasion for the assembled community, Party members, SA, and Hitler-Youth, to invoke and profess faith in National Socialist dogma.

55 Ibid., 6.

By withstanding the Jews,
I do the Lord's work.

Adolf Hitler, *Mein Kampf*

CHAPTER 7

APOCALYPSE

Leading National Socialists, and most importantly Hitler himself, had an apocalyptic view of the world. This vision was the extreme manifestation of National Socialist religiousness—or of the "political religion" of National Socialism—and is the only plausible explanation for the intention to destroy the Jews, which led to the holocaust. In this chapter these statements will be explained and substantiated.

First of all, it is important to note that the interpretation of National Socialist ideology as "apocalyptic" is not new. As early as 1938, in *The Political Religions*, Voegelin interpreted the conviction of National Socialists that they belonged to the chosen race and that the Jews, beyond all others, constituted an inferior "counter-race," as the expression of an apocalyptic view of the world. And he identified this view as one of the forms of modern apocalyptic interpretations of the world and history, pointing out that each apocalypse in the history of Europe "also created its own group of symbols for Satan."[1] During the war Sigmund Neuman characterized National Socialism as "messianic,"[2] and following the war Carl Joachim Friedrich described it as "chiliastic.".[3] And even Hans Mommsen, who otherwise rejects the concept of "political religion", confirmed the "chiliastic character of the National Socialist 'world view'"[4] in his seminal article "National Socialism," in *Meyers Enzyklopädisches Lexikon* (1976). Despite their various shades of meaning, the

1 Eric Voegelin, *The Political Regions* in *The Collected Works of Eric Voegelin*, vol. 5: *Modernity without Restraint*, ed. Manfred Henningsen (Columbia: University of Missouri Press, 2000), 19–74. Here, 61.

2 Sigmund Neumann, *Permanent Revolution: The Total State in a World at War* (New York: Harper and Brothers, 1942), 229.

3 Carl J. Friedrich, "The Unique Character of Totalitarian Society," in *Totalitarianism: Proceedings of a Conference Held at the American Academy of Arts and Sciences*, March,1953, ed. Carl J. Friedrich (Cambridge Mass.: Harvard University Press, 1954), 52.

4 Hans Mommsen, "Der Nationalsozialismus: Kumulative Radikalisierung und Selbstzerstörung des Regimes," in *Meyers Enzyklopädisches Lexikon.* vol. 16 (Mannheim, 1976), 786.

concepts messianic, chiliastic, and apocalyptic are often used as synonyms; I have chosen to use apocalyptic since it is the more comprehensive term.[5] It is not that I have tried to find the most impressive word to describe the phenomena; objective criteria demonstrate the correctness of placing the political religion of National Socialism in the Occidental tradition of apocalyptic thought, although the movement had separated itself from the tradition's religious roots and introduced new protagonists into the spiritual drama.

What does "apocalyptic" mean? For the Occidental tradition the essence of apocalypse is found in the last book of the New Testament, in the Revelation (Apocalypse) of Saint John. It begins with the sentence: "The Revelation (Greek: *apokalypsis*) of Jesus Christ, which God gave unto him, to show unto his servants things which must shortly come to pass [...]."[6] The word "apocalypse" was first used to describe the book itself. It later became a collective term for visions and prophecies related to the Revelation of St. John independent of whether they preceded it in time, like The Book of Daniel and many Jewish apocrypha, or whether they came later and, like most modern apocalypses, were no longer connected to Christianity. Finally "apocalypse" became the code word for the essential content of The Revelation of Saint John and related texts––namely, the destructive end of the world and the creation of a new one.

The Book of Daniel, the first apocalypse worked out in detail, offers consolation to pious Jews who were subject to the pressures of Hellenization in the Seleucid Empire during the second century B.C. The original salvation history (*Heilsgeschichte*) of Israel's exodus out of Egypt down to the Kingdom of David had ceased to be a living tradition and the promises, dating from the time of the Babylonian captivity, that the empire of Israel would rise again had not been fulfilled. Now that under Antiochus IV the very temple had been given over to the Hellenistic cult, the Jewish cult forbidden, and Orthodox Jews persecuted and killed, it seemed that the calamitous events of the world had reached a low point, indeed the absolute nadir, from which only one hope remained: that God would intervene and

5 See Klaus Vondung, *The Apocalypse in Germany*, 19–35.

6 *Rev* 1:1. This and subsequent quotations from the Bible: *King James Version of the Holy Bible Containing the Old and New Testaments* (Nashville: Thomas Nelson Publishers, 1984).

destroy the old world and its rulers and bring about a new era of promise. This was the message of The Book of Daniel.

For the Christians in the Roman Empire the tension between suffering in the world and the longing for salvation was, if anything, even greater. For the Messiah had already appeared and promised to return in the near future, thus mere worldly events were without meaning or purpose. The persecution of Christians and, finally, the demand that they worship Emperor Domitian only increased Christian impatience; the world could not become any more degenerate and evil than it already was. Toward the end of the first century John of Patmos prophesied that the end of suffering was near because salvation was at hand.

Thus the apocalyptic message was originally for those who longed for redemption because they were oppressed and persecuted, and because their suffering was so extreme that a change for the better no longer seemed possible. The apocalypse did not promise to simply improve the situation, but to radically transform reality and bring redemption through the destruction of the old, imperfect, and degenerate world.

In summary, the main structural characteristic of the apocalypse is the combination of destruction and renewal, of annihilation and redemption.[7] Apocalyptic thinking comes about in times of crisis in the minds of those who, in the entirety of existence—spiritual, social, and political—feel threatened, humiliated, oppressed, and persecuted. These feelings may have a real basis, but it is also possible that they may not accord with the facts, may be exaggerated, and indeed may rely on a false interpretation. But whatever the case, the apocalyptic visionary experiences the world as suffering and longs for redemption. At the same time the world appears to him to be so thoroughly degenerate and evil that he cannot imagine that by changes here and there or by reform anything substantial can be achieved. He believes that redemption can only come through the destruction of the old corrupt world and of those responsible for it. The apocalyptic thinker experiences the crisis as both acute and universal, sees the final judgment on it as inescapable, and believes that radical transformation will take place in the near future.

Thus, it is characteristic of the apocalypse to see first a strict and morally weighted dualism between the profoundly degenerate old world

7 For more on this subject, see Vondung, *The Apocalypse in Germany*.

and the perfect world of the future, between the "evil enemy" who is responsible for the present state of things and the elect who, although now just barely alive, will soon triumph over evil; second, the conviction that redemption must be preceded by the destruction of the old world and the annihilation of this evil enemy.

The apocalyptic writings that emerged between the second century B.C. and the second century A.D. established a rich and multi-formed literary tradition and influenced numerous streams of religious thought, which often gave expression to social protests or indeed pursued political goals. A striking common feature of these writings, whether Jewish or Christian, canonical or apocryphal, as well as those that had severed ties with their religious origins, is the language of violence. The Revelation of Saint John, the most important source of the Christian apocalyptic tradition, is the representative example: the vision's most striking images are of destruction. These terrifying scenes take up the bulk of the text and are far more compelling than the depiction of the immaculate New Jerusalem to come. Three great visions––that of the seven seals, seven trumpets, and seven bowls––describe in detail the incredible plagues that will come over the world and mankind before the Last Judgment is passed on Babylon, and the final battle against God's enemies takes place that will destroy Satan and his minions and be the occasion of Jerusalem's descent from Heaven.

The absoluteness of the apocalyptic vision makes the unlimited use of force appear necessary. This is in accord with the conception of the approaching final decision that resolves a bitter struggle in an incomparably horrible battle. The strict dualism of the apocalypse, the radical and morally weighted bifurcation between the deficient world and the hoped for new dispensation, is expressed in contrasting images of filth and purity and of darkness and light. The evil enemy is portrayed as a beast, a brutal, treacherous, nauseating and disgusting animal against which the use of violence is fully justified.

Of course, imagined violence does not necessarily lead to real violence, although violent acts are always preceded by imagined ones.[8] And the latter are all the more destructive where the intention to realize an apocalyptic

8 Cf. Wolfgang Sofsky, *Traktat über die Gewalt* (Frankfurt: S. Fischer Verlag, 1996); Wolfgang Sofsky, "Paradies der Grausamkeit," in *Frankfurter Allgemeine Zeitung*, (2.2.1999) 51.

interpretation of the world is present, especially when the threat posed by a supposed evil enemy is not real, is exaggerated, or merely exists in imagination. The religious and social groups in which the oldest Jewish and Christian visions of the apocalypse emerged were not activists, but quietists; in these visions it was God who intervened violently in order to destroy the evil enemy and his followers. The pious were content to imagine the violence that would be used against their oppressor. One might say they consoled themselves with fantasies of revenge. At a later time other interpretations emerged according to which the pious were permitted, indeed were obliged, to draw swords in order to carry out God's will. In the Middle Ages and early modern period some—not all—apocalyptic visionaries acted in accord with this belief.[9] Prominent examples are the Münster Anabaptists and Thomas Müntzer. In the city of Münster the "prophet" Jan Matthys demanded that all "Papists, Lutherans, and Sacramentists, and all those who did not accept the Anabaptist teachings, be killed."[10] And, later, the "prophet" Jan Bockelson, under his adopted name Johann van Leiden, King of the New Jerusalem (i.e. Münster), personally stabbed the smith Hubert Rüscher with a helbard because the latter had spoken of the prophet disrespectfully.[11] Thomas Müntzer wanted to kill the faithless because "unbelievers have no right to live."[12]

Some of the modern political apocalyptic movements that began with imagined violence also moved to real violence. They developed out of the tradition of religious apocalypse but broke with their roots. For this reason, the following important differences must be borne in mind.

Firstly, in the modern apocalypse it is no longer God who intervenes to bring salvation. This role is now taken by human beings and attributed to them exclusively. The protagonist in the apocalyptic drama is now a nation (as in German nationalism during the era of Napoleon and the First

9 Cf. Norman Cohn, *The Pursuit of the Millennium: Revolutionary Millenarians and Mystical Anarchists of the Middle Ages* (New York and Oxford: Oxford University Press, revised and expanded edition, 1970).

10 Richard van Dülmen, ed., *Das Täuferreich zu Münster 1534–1535. Berichte und Dokumente* (Munich: DTV, 1974), 71.

11 Ibid., 94f.

12 Thomas Müntzer, *Schriften und Briefe. Kritische Gesamtausgabe*, ed. Günther Franz (Gütersloh: Mohn, 1968), 261–262. Cf. 548.

World War), or a social class (as in the Marxist drama of history), or a race (as in National Socialism). The modern political apocalypse is neither of the "left" nor of the "right"; the paradigm can be filled with various ideological content.

Secondly, in the modern apocalyptic interpretation of the world the state of salvation is no longer thought of in terms of a Heavenly Jerusalem but of an earthly paradise. Unlike chiliastic speculation in the Middle Ages and in the early modern period, paradise is not ruled by Christ or one of his representatives, but by a nation or social class, or by a party as the class's avant-garde, or by a race, and a leader as the race's representative. The apocalypse is now completely world-immanent and if it still invokes "God" or the "Almighty" or "Providence," then it is for rhetorical purposes. The inner-worldly apocalypses suggest that a new vision can be realized and that violence will have to be used to establish it. Despite the inner-worldly character of these modern political movements, their structure, language, and content are so similar to the paradigm of religious apocalypse that they are justifiably termed "apocalypses."

In this sense the National Socialist interpretation of the world is an apocalyptic *Weltanschauung*. In *Mein Kampf* and in many speeches Hitler painted an apocalyptic picture of the world, one in which he undoubtedly believed, in which world history was determined by the struggle between two universal powers whose irreconcilable differences he generally expressed in the dualistic symbolism of light and darkness. He also believed that the decisive battle was near at hand in which the "deadly enemy of all light"[13] would be defeated. For Hitler, the "power of evil" was embodied in Jewishness, the "evil enemy of mankind"[14] which he blamed for the world's wrongs and held responsible for the threats and dangers that, in reality, were only figments of his imagination. For Hitler the Jews were the "real authors of all suffering"[15] and he believed that the salvation of the world depended on Germany winning the apocalyptic final battle against them. Other leading National Socialists shared this view. For example, Alfred Rosenberg believed in a world conspiracy of Jewish capitalism and

13 Adolf Hitler, *Mein Kampf*, vol. 2, 317, 320, 346, 752.

14 Ibid., 724.

15 Ibid.

Jewish Bolshevism against the "Northern race of light." He contributed to the growing fear of the end of civilization by developing the horrifying image of a Jewish world revolution, an "enormous planned messianic" attempt "to take revenge on the eternally alien character of Europeans, and not only of Europeans"; and he prophesied an apocalyptic struggle with a "decisive world-wide battle."[16] Like Hitler, he saw the dangerous avant garde of the Jews in "Jewish World-Bolshevism"[17] and, again like Hitler, he tried to turn the fear of the evil enemy into the will to destroy him: "Victory over the Bolshevist doctrine is only possible through a new *faith*, and out of this *Weltanschauung* through a willingness to act, and, *finally*, through the decisive act itself."[18]

The National Socialist apocalypse was also a vision of redemption. The destruction of the "evil enemy", i.e., the Jews, promised salvation. As Hitler wrote in *Mein Kampf*: "By withstanding the Jews, I do the Lord's work."[19] The invocation of "the Lord" was designed to make his Anti-Semitism palatable to Christians, and beyond that to legitimize the use of violence. Hitler made it crystal clear that the National Socialists should engage in violence and the violent vocabulary he used to justify it is striking. He does not speak of "opponents" but of "foes," and "battle," "ruthless attacks," and "extermination."[20] In Hitler's apocalyptic view of the world, unlimited violence against Jews is justified because Germany's fate, indeed the fate of mankind, depends upon the evil enemy being destroyed. In Hitler's words: "If our people and our State succumb to these blood and money hungry tyrants of the peoples, the whole earth will be trapped in the monster's tentacles; but if Germany can free itself from its grip the power of this greatest danger to the nations will be broken."[21]

Further justification for mercilessly using violence against Jews was supplied by heaping abusive images on them and identifying them with

16 Alfred Rosenberg, *Der entscheidende Weltkampf. Rede des Reichsleiters Alfred Rosenberg auf dem Parteikongreß in Nürnberg 1936* (Munich: Münchner Buchgewerbehaus M. Müller, 1936), 2–4, 12–13.

17 Cf. Hitler, *Mein Kampf*, 752.

18 Rosenberg, *Der entscheidende Weltkampf*, 13 (Italics in the original spaced).

19 Hitler, *Mein Kampf*, 70.

20 Ibid., 371

21 Ibid., 703.

the apocalyptic beast of the abyss. Hitler's images of "foulness and refuse"[22] were taken up by Goebbels who noted in his diary: "The Jew is indeed the anti-Christ of world history. One can hardly find oneself in all this filth of lies, refuse, blood, and bestial ferocity."[23] Rosenberg described the "final decisive struggle" as a battle against filth: "Either we [...] strengthen our will for a purifying struggle, or the last Germanic western values of civilization and ordered statehood will sink under the filthy human flood of 'cosmopolitan' cities."[24] In order to stamp the Jew with the image of being an especially dangerous and repulsive "evil enemy of humanity" and to make the program to eradicate him appear as a policy of "disinfection," the Jew was associated with vermin. The 1940 propaganda film, *The Eternal Jew*, displayed the spread of the Jews through Europe with a map that was continually overlaid with images of swarming rats; in *Mein Kampf* Hitler had already compared Jews to a "horde of rats."[25]

Naturally, the actual transition from imaginary to *de facto* violence, to massacres and mass murder, requires additional explanation. Two recent noteworthy studies have analyzed in detail the process that led to the 20th century's large scale violence and genocide. The historians Jörg Baberowski and Anselm Doering-Manteuffel compare the murderous terror of Nazi Germany with Stalin's. The French political scientist Jacques Sémelin compares the massacre and genocide of Nazi Germany with those in Bosnia and Rwanda. Both studies show that the transition from imaginary, or indeed proclaimed, violence to actual violence requires several pre-conditions. Among others, the authors identify the following for the mass murder of Jews: the 1914–1918 experience of war that had a brutalizing effect on the soldiers and left them numb to mass suffering and dying; the ideological indoctrination following defeat in war, and the legend of having been "stabbed in the back." The authors find the most important pre-condition in spiritual-intellectual pre-requisites––namely, a type of "pre-knowledge"

22 Ibid., 331.

23 Fröhlich, *Die Tagebücher von Joseph Goebbels*, Part I, vol. 1/II (June 26, 1926) (Munich: Saur, 2005), 99.

24 Alfred Rosenberg, *Der Mythos des 20. Jahrhunderts. Eine Wertung der seelisch-geistigen Gestaltenkämpfe unserer Zeit* (Munich: Hoheneichen, 53–54th printing,1935), 82.

25 Hitler, *Mein Kampf,* 331.

or "context of meaning" whose thought "anticipates" mass murder.[26] For Baberowski and Doering-Manteuffel these pre-requisites include "ideologies of Manichaean salvation,"[27] whereby the criteria for the use of this term is obviously the ideologies' dualistic worldview. Indeed this dualism is the only criteria the authors have for justifying the use of the term "Manichean," for there is no historical connection to the Manichean religion that disappeared in the 14th century.[28] However, in contrast, there is now a 2,000 year uninterrupted tradition of apocalyptic interpretations of the world and history including, beginning in the 18th century, secular political ones. Just a few years prior to Stalin and Hitler developing their worldviews and attaining political power there was an abundance of apocalyptic interpretations of World War I and the nationalist and socialist revolutions that followed. It was in this spiritual milieu that Stalin and Hitler received their ideas; for this reason their views of the world had more to do with the apocalyptic tradition than with Manichaeism.

Two elements are essential for the development of an apocalyptic interpretation of the world and history. First, there are occasions of concrete experience, primarily of crisis; and second, there is the virulence of traditional patterns of interpretation with the help of which such experiences are interpreted. For Hitler and many of his contemporaries the outbreak of war in 1914 produced feelings of elation which were often interpreted in terms like the following: "For years now Germany has been surrounded"[29]

26 Jörg Baberowski and Anselm Doering-Manteuffel, *Ordnung durch Terror. Gewaltexzesse und Vernichtung im nationalsozialistischen und im stalinistischen Imperium* (Bonn: Dietz, 2006), 16, 28. Jaques Sémelin, *Purify and Destroy: The Political Uses of Massacre and Genocide* (New York: Columbia University Press, 2009). Quoted here according to the German translation, *Säubern und Vernichten. Die Politik der Massaker und Völkermorde* (Hamburg: Hamburger ed., 2007), 68, 263.

27 Baberowski and Doering-Manteuffel, *Ordnung durch Terror*, 16.

28 Since the philosophical and theological discussions of the 17th Century, the term "Manichean" or "Manichaeism" has generally been used—as Baberowski and Doering-Manteuffel use it—as a synonym for dualism. The term is used by those who wish to distance themselves from it or as part of a polemic against others.

29 Reinhard Buchwald, ed., *Der Heilige Krieg. Gedichte aus dem Beginn des Kampfes* (Jena: Diederichs, 1914), 70 (Cäsar Flaischlen).

and exposed to the "yellow slime of livid hate,"[30] now it is called upon to pass judgment on its enemies. These were described as "beasts," "dragons," and "vipers," and identified with the "devil" and "Anti-Christ." "Final victory" would bring Germany a "new Reich" and "redemption" to the world.[31] But the increasing misery of war and its suffering and death, resulting finally in Germany's defeat, induced many young men, primarily socialist-leaning intellectuals, artists, and writers like Ernst Bloch, Ernst Toller, and Kurt Hiller to interpret their experiences and color their hopes with a different apocalyptic vision. The old bourgeois world that had so bestially torn itself apart deserved to be destroyed completely. Indeed, it had to be eradicated so that a clean slate could be made for humanity to re-create the world as an earthly paradise.[32] The fact that the world had grown so chaotic, murderous, and evil seemed to point to the inevitability of apocalyptic intervention in the near future. Thus in 1921 Ernst Bloch concluded: "It is not possible that such a dark world could come *over us*, were there not an absolute storm, a central light, in our immediate future."[33] He believed that he could discern "the birth pangs of the world's final revolution." This revolution would bring the "absolute transformation" that would turn "all things to paradise," bring about the Third Reich, and create the "new man" and the "new world."[34]

But the nationalists and the National Socialists also had an apocalyptic interpretation of Germany's defeat in 1918 and of the conditions that followed. The feeling that one had reached a low point in world history was not merely the result of the lost war, material suffering, and social insecurity.

30 Ibid., 2 (Gerhart Hauptmann).

31 For the source of these quotations and numerous others, see Klaus Vondung, "Geschichte als Weltgericht. Genesis und Degradation einer Symbolik," in *Kriegserlebnis. Der Erste Weltkrieg in der literarischen Gestaltung und symbolischen Deutung der Nationen* Klaus Vondung, ed. (Göttingen: Vandenhoeck and Ruprecht, 1980), 66.

32 Kurt Hiller, "Philosophie des Ziels," in *Das Ziel. Aufrufe zum tätigen Geist* (Munich und Berlin: Georg Müller Verlag, 1916), 187–217. Here 196.

33 Ernst Bloch, *Thomas Münzer als Theologe der Revolution* (Berlin: Kurt Wolff, 1921), 296 (Italics in the original spaced).

34 Ernst Bloch, *Thomas Münzer*, 150–151, 297; Ernst Bloch, *Geist der Utopie* (Berlin: Cassirer,1923), 209, 325.

The atomization of society and its norms and the collapse of values and institutions that had once given life meaning and stability led to a feeling that life was fundamentally meaningless and thus to complete disorientation. This was a situation that threatened not only social and political life but existence itself. For example, for the writer Rudolf G. Bindung, who in 1933 in an open letter to Romain Rolland declared his faith in National Socialism,[35] the experiences of deficiency and loss combined to produce a feeling of "non-existence" that "tortured his soul."[36] In the mid-1920s the young Joseph Goebbels confided his world weariness and feelings of personal inadequacy in his diary: "Despair! Skepticism! Collapse! I no longer know what's up or down"(June 30th, 1924); "Oh the ocean of pain in this world! Despair and destruction!" (April 20th, 1925); "Oh, this horrible world!" (September 3rd, 1925); "Hopelessly lonely. I stand on the verge of despair [...] horrible desolation! Mother help me! I can't go on!" (September 4th, 1925).[37] In the apocalyptic interpretation of these experiences the Jews were denounced as "the real cause of all suffering."[38]

In his book Jacques Sémelin speaks occasionally of the "apocalyptic discourse" in Nazi Germany[39] but associates the concept only with its destructive results. But, as a matter of fact, Sémelin and Baberowski, as well as Doering-Manteuffel, list almost all of the criteria which—beyond the appearance of Manichean dualism—are characteristic of the inner-worldly apocalypse, and as I have demonstrated are present in National Socialism: from the belief that the Jews are a threat, to the ideology's typical "categorical absoluteness," the denunciation of the enemy as "bestial," identifying him with filth and chaos, the invocation of a so-called "higher law" that provides a quasi-justification for genocide, right up to the goal of creating a society of "unity," "purity," and "homogeneity" for which Baberowski and Doering-Manteuffel use the term "an order of paradise."[40] Indeed, for the title of his book Sémelin takes the two most

35 *Sechs Bekenntnisse zum neuen Deutschlandholz*, See also above p. 24f.

36 Ibid., 17.

37 Frölich, *Die Tagebücher von Joseph Goebbels,* Part I, vol. 1/I, 157, 295, 349–350.

38 Hitler, *Mein Kampf*, 724.

39 Sémelin, *Säubern und Vernichten*, 320, cf. 87.

40 Baberowski and Doering-Manteuffel, *Ordnung durch Terror*, 16, 47–48, 66; Sémelin, *Säubern und Vernichten,* 45, 51, 92, 280.

important characteristics of apocalyptic actionism: *Purify and Destroy* (*Purifier et détruire*).

Thus one can say that these two important books deal with the political apocalypses of the 20th century, but without using the term that best describes them: both works characterize the apocalyptic images of the world in their various ideological trappings, and then trace and explain the transition from the apocalyptic imagination to the use of violence. In addition, they enable us to identify the particular nature of apocalyptic violence. Its main characteristic is not, as one might think, excessive cruelty, although naturally apocalyptic violence can be very extreme: Wolfgang Sofsky has demonstrated convincingly that the perpetrators of sadistic violence require no special motivation or justification for their acts,[41] but apocalyptic violence requires motives and justifications. Its main characteristic is its preknowledge, something Timothy Snyder, who correctly saw the phenomenon though vaguely, termed "a universal prejudice."[42] More precisely it is a fundamental "context of meaning," an apocalyptic interpretation of the world with its corresponding consequences. According to this kind of interpretation there is an irreconcilable enmity between the representatives of the New Society and the evil enemy and the notion predominates that the enemy must be destroyed in a final battle that will take place in the immediate future. The apocalyptic interpretation of the world turns the enemy—"the power of evil"— into an abstract category and he is denied a human face. Additionally, equating the enemy with beasts and vermin makes him appear sub-human or non-human. The combination of these interpretations makes it possible that the violence used against him takes on the categorical, abstract, bureaucratic quality characteristic of the mechanized mass murder of the Jews in death camps.

There is no necessary connection between motive and act; apocalyptic visions do not lead inevitably to violence. Between what is imagined and what is actually implemented lies the sphere of human freedom to act or desist from action. Also, the apocalyptic violence envisioned by individuals

41 Sofsky, *Traktat über die Gewalt*; Ibid., "Paradies der Grausamkeit."

42 "Vierzehn Millionen Opfer waren nicht überraschend. Im Gespräch: Die Historiker Ian Kershaw und Timothy Snyder," in *Frankfurter Allgemeine Zeitung*, 19 September 2012, N. 4.

who do not have the power to act differs from the violence implemented by those who do. The organized mass murder could not have been carried out had there not been institutional power—a regime—that made the decision and had the administrative and organizational structure to implement it. In the case of National Socialism, the process of violence against Jews was progressively radicalized. It began with legal discrimination and the segregation of persons who were identified as evil enemies: imposing restrictions upon them, intimidating them, taking their property, physically attacking them, and finally committing the first acts of murder. During the war "legal vacuums"[43] were established in the East in which genocide could be organized. There was also a process of "cumulative radicalization," as Hans Mommsen called it,[44] a "step by step developing process of the radicalization of political racism [...] that inevitably leads to the Shoah."[45] But the process itself cannot explain the end it led to, rather the specific process was guided by a general intention. For even if at the time when Hitler wrote *Mein Kampf* he did not have in mind the "Final Solution of the Jewish Question" in death camps, this form of genocide could only take place because the intention to remove the Jews had been present from the beginning; it governed the direction in which measures against the Jews were taken[46] and at the same time provided the rationale and justification for such acts. Neither the perpetrators in the bureaucracy (*Schreibtischtäter*) nor the death camp personnel who physically committed the murders acted autonomously. Besides pointing to orders that they had to carry out, they justified their actions by appealing to a system of values whose center is the apocalyptic world view of Hitler and other National Socialist leaders.

43 Baberowski and Doering-Manteuffel, *Ordnung durch Terror*, 38, 48.

44 Mommsen, "Der Nationalsozialismus," esp. 789–790 and 792.

45 Hans Mommsen, "Forschungskontroversen zum Nationalsozialismus," in *Aus Politik und Zeitgeschichte* 57 (2007), 15.

46 The positions of the "intentionalists" and the "functionalists" do not necessarily contradict one another, and can be seen as complementary. Hans Mommsen, who originally took a decisively "functionalist" position in opposition to the "intentionalists" Raul Hilberg, Yehuda Bauer, Saul Friedländer, Eberhard Jäckel, and others, conceded in 2007: "In the meantime research has brought the positions closer together." Mommsen, "Forschungskontroversen zum Nationalsozialismus," 17.

Baberowski and Doering-Manteuffel have shown just how important it is for the perpetrators to be able to appeal to a "higher law"[47] in order to justify their actions. And Sémelin has demonstrated that mass murder can be most effectively carried out where it is morally sanctioned.[48] Dyed in the wool, National Socialists adopted the values of the apocalyptic world view of Hitler and his followers as their own moral principles and raised them to the status of articles of faith. Herman Lübbe explained how the perpetrators rationalized mass murder by the appeal to a higher moral law which they accepted as a matter of faith: "To bloody one's hands for a higher cause is not the way a cynic rationalizes his horrible deeds, but how a believer does whose moral common sense has been shattered by ideology and who has reformulated his disorientation in categories of faith in inner-worldly salvation."[49] As we have seen, the articles of faith of the National Socialist apocalyptic world view were constantly articulated by Hitler and other leading Nazis: they were visualized in Party rallies and celebrations, repeated and disseminated by faithful National Socialist intellectuals—and not just by Party propagandists, but by university professors, journalists, and teachers. Even if the "believers" among the intellectuals were not identical with the perpetrators, and not all the perpetrators necessarily faithful National Socialists, the National Socialist world view determined the nature of the entire society. It created the dominant climate of opinion and established the moral standards of conduct and action. And if, as one of these articles of faith maintained, the Jews were the "evil enemy of mankind" and the well-being of society––and therefore the salvation of all good human beings––depended upon the destruction of this power of evil, then it was a logical step to take action against them. Even for the perpetrators who were not necessarily among the faithful, but merely obtuse underlings bereft of moral standards, or as Lübbe put it, those whose "moral common sense had been shattered by ideology," the article of faith concerning the evil enemy of mankind provided them with the semblance of a formal justification for their deeds.

47 Baberowski and Doering-Manteuffel, *Ordnung durch Terror*, 48.

48 Sémelin, *Säubern und Vernichten*, 280.

49 Hermann Lübbe, "Totalitäre Rechtgläubigkeit. Das Heil und der Terror," in *Heilserwartung und Terror. Politische Religionen des 20. Jahrhunderts,* ed. Hermann Lübbe (Düsseldorf: Patmos, 1995), 9.

This mind set is especially well illustrated in the self-image of Rudolf Höß, commandant of the Auschwitz death camp from 1940 until 1943. In his autobiographical notes, which he wrote in prison after 1945, he proved himself to be, as the editor Martin Broszat described him, a man of "zealously eager conscientiousness" who "always did his duty, both as an executioner and as a confessed delinquent, who lived only at second-hand and effaced his own person," and who nevertheless elevated this "robot-like diligence to a 'noble' concept of virtue" and thus, in his own mind, was "indeed eminently 'moral.'"[50] Höß completely internalized the dogma of Anti-Semitism. For him it was an "earnest Anti-Semitism" without personal hatred.[51] For himself and his accomplices he justified the necessity "that hundreds of thousands of women and children would have to be killed" with the argument of the apocalyptic interpretation of the world, and in almost the same words that he knew from Hitler: "[T]he destruction of the Jews is necessary in order that Germany and our descendents will be free of their most tenacious adversary for all time."[52] Accordingly, Himmler's orders that "the Jews are the eternal enemies of the German people and must be exterminated,"[53] was Gospel for Höß. "His principle orders in the name of the *Fuehrer* were holy."[54]

*

The apocalypse promises redemption through destruction. This is a fatal connection, also in Judeo-Christian apocalypses, and is the reason why many Jews and Christians are skeptical of apocalyptic visions. At least in the original Jewish and Christian apocalypses the Last Judgment is placed in the hands of God. The pious, to whom salvation has been promised, and who are called upon to be patient and endure suffering, can draw consolation from the apocalypse only as long as God has not inter-

50 Martin Broszat, "Einleitung," in Rudolf Höß, *Kommandant in Auschwitz. Autobiographische Aufzeichnungen.* ed. Martin Broszat (Munich: DTV, 21st edition, 2008), 13, 19, 21.

51 Höß, *Kommandant in Auschwitz*, 168, 170.

52 Ibid., 197.

53 Ibid., 237.

54 Ibid., 187, 223.

vened. In *The Book of Daniel* the Jews Schadrach, Meschach, and Abednego were hurled into the fiery furnace because they refused to obey Nebuchadnezzar's command to worship the image of gold.[55] Daniel himself was thrown into the lion's den because he prayed to his God and placed God's laws over the decree of King Darius that no one was to petition anything of a god or man but only of the king.[56] Both of these histories were clearly intended to serve as a model for Jews living under the Seleucid Empire, for Antioch IV had also banned the Jewish cult. In *The Book of Revelation* John admonishes the Christian community not to bow to the power of evil, represented by the Roman Empire and its laws, but to keep faith with God.[57] Of course, in both cases the violation of the law of the earthly rulers and keeping God's higher law brought punishment, suffering, and even death.

In the National Socialist apocalypse the faithful also invoked a higher law, primarily the "racial law" that is at the heart of National Socialist faith. But here the invocation served the purpose of justifying the persecution and killing of *others* who were not in a position to defend themselves. The branding of Jews as the power of evil and the source of all suffering was an act of psychological projection. Raising Blood and *Volk* to sacred goods and elevating racial laws to the supreme law governing praxis served to justify every imaginable means of eradicating the evil enemy. And the idea, induced by self-hypnosis, that one has the power to determine the welfare or suffering of the entire world stirs and unleashes tumultuous feelings. In 1934 the young National Socialist poet Kurt Eggers wrote:

> Place fire under the cauldrons
> and let the flames crackle,
> the fire under the cauldrons,
> the fires that unlock the power,
> liberate us too.[58]

55 Daniel 3:20.

56 Daniel 6:7.

57 Revelation 2 and 13:9.

58 Kurt Eggers, *Sturmsignale. Revolutionäre Sprechchöre* (Leipzig: Strauch, 1934, 2nd edition, 1936), 18–19.

In his study, *The Political Religions*, Voegelin virtually subjects the poems of Gerhard Schumann to a psychoanalytic interpretation and pursues the "politico-religious excitations" into their climax in the "blood lust of the deed."[59] Neither Eggers nor Schumann murdered Jews, neither before 1938 nor after. And in the spring of 1938, before the November 9th pogrom, hardly anyone could imagine that the persecution of the Jews would culminate in mass murder. Voegelin's emotional expression, "blood lust of the deed," reverberated with the knowledge of the violent excesses that Jews had already been subjected to since 1933, and about which one could inform oneself in the Vienna newspapers, and indeed in German newspapers, a fact testified to eloquently in the pages of Karl Kraus' *Fackel*.[60]

Between the "blood lust of the deed" and an Anti-Semitism "devoid of hate," there is a broad spectrum of motives that led human beings to torment, persecute, and murder Jews. Naturally, in addition to the "earnest Anti-Semites" among the bureaucratic murderers who were purportedly free of hate, there was also a hate filled Anti-Semitism; Hitler, but also Himmler, Goebbels, and Rosenberg felt deep hatred toward the Jews as their writings and speeches clearly demonstrate.[61] And there was also a widespread "muffled and vague Anti-Semitism," as Götz Aly, following Jacob Wassermann, termed the unreflected resentment toward the Jews that stemmed from religious anti-Judaism.[62] Undoubtedly there was also sadism, and there were the underlings made up of "entirely normal men"[63] who did not have the moral strength to free themselves from the web of orders and servile obedience. Finally, there was envy toward more competent and

59 Voeglin, *The Political Religions,* in *The Collected Works,* vol. 5, 67.

60 *Die Fackel,* nr. 890–905. "Warum die Fackel nicht erscheint," in 36. *Jg*. (End of July 1934). The full text appeared after the war as *Die Dritte Walpurgisnacht* (Munich: Kösel, 1952).

61 Hitler became a "fanatical Anti-Semite" after the First World War, although when he discusses his feelings toward the Jews in *Mein Kampf* he claims that it was during his stay in Vienna "that I slowly began to hate them." Hitler, *Mein Kampf*, 67, 69.

62 Götz Aly, *Warum die Deutschen? Warum die Juden? Gleichheit, Neid und Rassenhass 1800–1933* (Frankfurt: Fischer, 2011), 258–262.

63 Cf. Christopher R. Browning, *Ganz normale Männer. Das Reserve-Polizeibatallion 101 und die "Endlösung" in Polen* (Reinbeck: Rowohlt, 1993).

successful Jewish scientists, doctors, lawyers, writers and journalists, and toward well-to-do entrepreneurs, merchants, and bankers. Götz Aly has described the genesis of this syndrome and considers social envy to be an essential source of German Anti-Semitism. These, along with the fact that after 1933 many Germans could enrich themselves on Jewish property and take the places that Jews had been forced to vacate, are convincing reasons for the widespread silent approval of the persecution of the Jews.[64]

The motives sketched above provide plausible explanations for why the Jews suffered discrimination, were dispossessed of their property, and driven from their country; indeed they can explain why the Jews were mistreated and individuals murdered. But they do not explain why systematic and mechanized mass murder took place. Yet the Holocaust becomes plausible—in a perverse way—when these various motives are taken together and at the same time justified by the apocalyptic image of the evil enemy of mankind.

64 Aly, *Warum die Deutschen?*, esp. 7–14, 262–267, 288–301.

AFTERWORD

This book summarizes decades of research on the religious aspects of National Socialism. In the beginning––now almost a half century ago––when my studies first turned to this period my focus was not on religious phenomena. But as I looked for an interesting topic for my dissertation in German literature I discovered the curious genre of "choral poetry" (*chorische Dichtung*), a literary form that combines drama and lyric poetry. Choral poetry was cultivated primarily in the Third Reich and generally by younger writers. A closer look revealed that it was used almost exclusively in the manifold forms of National Socialist celebration. Choral poetry supplied the liturgical texts for events of cultic character. From Eric Voegelin, my teacher in political science, I had learned not to limit the scope of my research to the bounds set by an academic discipline, but to conduct problem-oriented research and to insure that the method of investigation was appropriate to the nature of the object to be studied. Because the research object was not limited to a body of texts, along with methods of text interpretation, other interpretative methods also had to be used. In line with these considerations the dissertation I submitted to the Philosophy Faculty of the University of Munich in the winter semester of 1968–1969 was concerned with cult phenomena in the Third Reich as expressions of what—following Eric Voegelin—I called the "political religion" of National Socialism. In addition to the interpretation of choral poems in their function as liturgical texts the dissertation investigated the types and structures of the events and celebrations in which the texts appeared and the venues where they took place. It also examined the intentions of the offices that directed the staging of National Socialist ceremonies, the course and development of such festivities during the Third Reich, the cult's social function, the state of mind of those who carried out the celebrations, and the general public's response. The methods of investigation were developed in accord with the structure of the objects to be studied and in response to the questions that the research generated. Archive resources and interviews, for example with Albert Speer, completed the material basis of the published dissertation.[1]

From that time until today the theme of the political religion of National Socialism has held my interest. At conferences and in numerous articles I have presented my research into other manifestations of the phenomenon and offered new perspectives for studying the religious aspects of National Socialism. Over time this field of research began to overlap with one that, at first, had seemed to me to be unrelated to it. However, during 1972–1973 I was able to spend almost two years conducting research at Stanford University. I wanted to study the extensive archive material at the university's Hoover Institution on War, Revolution, and Peace in order to examine the connections between linguistic extremism and social violence. I began with a study of World War I materials—war poems, sermons, and academic addresses—and soon realized that all of these texts employed apocalyptic symbols, and that their interpretations of the war were based on apocalyptic patterns of thought. After my first publications on the topic the German Apocalypse 1914 (*Deutsche Apokalypse 1914*), I undertook studies of the apocalyptic interpretation of the world and history in the philosophy, politics and literature of various epochs, and also discovered that Hitler—and other leading National Socialists—had an apocalyptic understanding of the world. In 1988 I published the systematic treatment of the apocalyptic tradition in Germany.[2] In the ensuing period I saw more and more the necessity of linking the interpretation of National Socialism as a political religion to the apocalyptic tradition. In numerous articles I developed the thesis that National Socialism's apocalyptic world view was the extreme manifestation of its political religion and, in the final analysis, the only plausible explanation for the intention of exterminating the Jews that led to the holocaust.[3]

1 Klaus Vondung, *Magie und Manipulation. Ideologischer Kult und politische Religion des Nationalsozialismus* (Göttingen: Vandenhoeck and Ruprecht, 1971).

2 Klaus Vondung, *Die Apokalypse in Deutschland* (Munich: DTV, 1988). English: *The Apocalypse in Germany* (Columbia: University of Missouri Press, 2000).

3 Recent publications: Klaus Vondung, "What Insights Do We Gain from Interpreting National Socialism as a Political Religion?" in *The Sacred in Twentieth-Century Politics. Essays in Honour of Professor Stanley G. Payne,* Roger Griffin, Robert Mallett, John Tortorice, eds. (Houndmills, Basingstoke: Macmillan, 2008), 107–118; id., "Der Preis des Paradieses: Gewalt in Apoka-

Much of what I presented in these articles and books over a period of several decades has gone into this volume. However the need to sum up the results of this work also compelled me to take a fresh look at the phenomenon and instead of developing a systematic presentation under the category of political religion, a concept that does not always accurately describe National Socialist reality, I wanted to provide exemplary analyses of the various aspects of the forms of religion that are found in National Socialism. I believe that the motivational center of these various forms is the longing for redemption. This motivational center expressed itself in various ways and each chapter examines one of the religious phenomena that manifests itself in National Socialism.

lypse und Utopie," in *Utopie und Apokalypse in der Moderne,* Reto Sorg and Stefan Bodo Würffel eds. (Munich: Fink, 2010), 33–45; id., "Debatten um den Holocaust und das Deutungskonzept der 'politischen Religion,'" in *Zeitschrift für Literaturwissenschaft und Linguistik* (LiLi), *Jg*. 10, Heft 157 (2010), "Deutsche Debatten," 9–22.

BIBLIOGRAPHY

Albert, Karl. *Einführung in die philosophische Mystik*. Darmstadt: Wiss. Buchgesellschaft, 1996.

Aly, Götz. *Hitlers Volksstaat. Raub, Rassenkrieg und nationaler Sozialismus, revised and expanded.* Frankfurt am Main: S. Fischer, 2006. English translation: *Hitler's Beneficiaries: Plunder, Racial War, and the Nazi Welfare State.* London: Picador, 2008.

———. *Warum die Deutschen? Warum die Juden? Gleichheit, Neid und Rassenhass 1800–1933*. Frankfurt am Main: S. Fischer, 2011; English translation: *Why the Germans? Why the Jews?: Envy, Race Hatred, and the Prehistory of the Holocaust.* London: Picador, 2015.

Arendt, Hannah. *The Origins of Totalitarianism.* New York: Meridian, 1955; German translation: *Elemente und Ursprünge totaler Herrschaft.* Frankfurt am Main: Europäische Verlagsanstalt, 1962.

Baberowski, Jörg and Anselm Doering-Manteufel. *Ordnung durch Terror. Gewaltexzesse und Vernichtung im nationalsozialistischen und im stalinistischen Imperium*. Bonn: J. H. W. Dietz, 2006.

Bärsch, Claus-Ekkehard. *Die politische Religion des Nationalsozialismus. Die religiösen Dimensionen der NS-Ideologie in den Schriften von Dietrich Eckart, Joseph Goebbels, Alfred Rosenberg und Adolf Hitler.* Munich: Fink, 2002.

Behrenbeck, Sabine. *Der Kult um die toten Helden. Nationalsozialistische Mythen, Riten und Symbole*. Vierow bei Greifswald: SH Verlag, 1996.

Berg, Nicolas. *Der Holocaust und die westdeutschen Historiker. Erforschung und Erinnerung*. Göttingen: Wallstein Verlag, 2002. English translation: *The Holocaust and the West German Historians: Historical Interpretation and Autobiographical Memory.* Madison: University of Wisconsin Press, 2015.

Boberach, Heinz, ed. *Meldungen aus dem Reich 1938–1945. Die geheimen Lageberichte des Sicherheitsdienstes der SS.* 17 volumes. Herrsching: Pawlak, 1984.

Bollmus, Reinhard. *Das Amt Rosenberg und seiner Gegner. Studien zum Machtkampf im nationalsozialistischen Herrschaftssystem.* Stuttgart: DVA, 1970.

Browning, Christoper R. *Ganz normale Männer. Das Reserve Polizeibataillon 101 und die "Endlösung" in Polen.* Reinbeck: Rowohlt, 1993. English original: *Ordinary Men: Reserve Police Battalion 101 and the Final Solution in Poland*. New York: Harper Collins, 1992.

Browning, Christoper R. *Die Entfesselung der "Endlösung." Nationalsozialistische Judenpolitik 1939–1942.* Munich: Propyläen, 2003. English original: *The Origins of the Final Solution: The Evolution of Nazi Jewish Policy, September 1939–March 1942*. With contributions by Jürgen Matthäus. Lincoln: University of Nebraska Press, 2004.

Bucher, Rainer. *Hitlers Theologie.* Würzburg: Echter, 2008. English translation: *Hitler's Theology.* New York and London: Continuum International Publishing Group, 2011.

Burleigh, Michael J. *Die Zeit des Nationalsozialismus. Eine Gesamtdarstellung*. 2nd edition. Frankfurt am Main: Fischer, 2000. English original: *The Third Reich. A New History.* London: Pan Macmillan, 2000.

–––––. *Irdische Mächte, göttliches Heil. Die Geschichte des Kampfes zwischen Politik und Religion von der Französischen Revolution bis zur Gegenwart.* Munich: DVA, 2008. English original: *Earthly Powers. The Clash of Religion and Politics in Europe, from the French Revolution to the Great War.* New York: Harper Perennial, 2007.

Burrin, Philippe. *Warum die Deutschen? Antisemitismus, Nationalsozialismus, Genozid.* Berlin: Propyläen, 2004. French original: *Ressentiment et apocalypse. Essai sur l'antisémitisme nazi.* Paris: Le Seuil, 2004.

Albert Camus. *The Rebel: An Essay on Man in Revolt.* New York: Vintage Books, 1956.

Cohn, Norman. *The Pursuit of the Millennium: Revolutionary Millenarians and Mystical Anarchists of the Middle Ages.* Revised and expanded edition. Oxford: Oxford University Press, 1970.

Van Dülmen, Richard, ed. *Das Täuferreich zu Münster 1534–1535. Berichte und Dokumente.* Munich: DTV, 1974.

Durkheim, Emile. *Die elementaren Formen des religiösen Lebens.* Frankfurt am Main: Suhrkamp, 1981. English translation (of the French original):

The Elementary Forms of Religious Life. Oxford: Oxford University Press, 2008.

Eliade, Mircea. *Das Heilige und das Profane. Vom Wesen des Religiösen*. Hamburg: Rowohlt, 1957. English translation (of the French original): *The Sacred and the Profane*. Boston: Houghton Mifflin, 1968.

Fest, Joachim C. *Hitler. Eine Biographie*. Frankfurt am Main, Berlin, Vienna: Ullstein, 1973. English translation: *Hitler*. New York: Harcourt, 1973.

Flacke, Monika, ed. *Mythen der Nationen. Ein europäisches Panorama*. Ausstellungskatalog. Berlin: Deutsches Historisches Museum, 1998.

Friedländer, Saul. *Die Jahre der Vernichtung. Das Dritte Reich und die Juden 1939–1945*. Munich: C. H. Beck, 2006. English original: *The Years of Extermination: Nazi Germany and the Jews, 1939–1945*. New York: Harper Collins, 2007.

Friedlander, Henry. *Der Weg zum NS-Genozid. Von der Euthanasie zur Endlösung*. Darmstadt: Wissenschaftliche Buchgesellschaft, 1997. English original: *The Origins of Nazi Genocide: From Euthanasia to The Final Solution*. Chapel Hill: University of North Carolina Press, 1995.

Friedrich, Carl Joachim, ed. *Totalitarianism: Proceedings of a Conference Held at the American Academy of Arts and Sciences, March 1953*. Cambridge, Massachusetts: Harvard University Press, 1954.

Friedrich, Carl Joachim and Brzezinski, Zbigniew. *Totalitarian Dictatorship and Autocracy*. Cambridge, Massachusetts: Harvard University Press, 1956.

Fröhlich, Elke, ed. *Die Tagebücher von Joseph Goebbels. Sämtliche Fragmente*. Munich: Saur, 1987.

Gamm, Hans-Jochen. *Der braune Kult. Das Dritte Reich und seine Ersatzreligion. Ein Beitrag zur politischen Bildung*. Hamburg: Rütten and Loening, 1962.

Gentile, Emilio. *Le religioni della politica: Fra democrazie e totalitarismi*. Rome and Bari: Laterza, 2001. English translation: *Politics as Religion*. Princeton: Princeton University Press, 2006.

Glaser, Hermann. *Das Dritte Reich. Anspruch und Wirklichkeit*. 4th ed. Freiburg: Herder, 1963.

Goodrick-Clarke, Nicholas. *Die okkulten Wurzeln des Nationalsozialismus*. Wiesbaden: Marix, 2004. English original: *The Occult Roots of Nazism: Secret*

Aryan Cults and Their Influence on Nazi Ideology; The Ariosophists of Austria and Germany, 1890–1935. New York: New York University Press, 1992.

Gray, John. *Politik der Apokalypse. Wie Religion die Welt in die Krise stürzt.* Stuttgart: Klett-Cotta, 2009. English original: *Black Mass*. New York: Farrar, Straus, Giroux, 2007.

Griffin, Roger, Robert Mallett, John Tortorice, eds. *The Sacred in Twentieth-Century Politics. Essays in Honour of Professor Stanley G. Price.* Houndmills, Basingstoke: MacMillan, 2008.

Haas, Alois M. *Mystik im Kontext.* Munich: Fink, 2004.

Heer, Friedrich. *Der Glaube des Adolf Hitler. Anatomie einer politischen Religiosität*. Munich and Eßlingen: Bechtle, 1968.

Heiber, Helmut. *Joseph Goebbels.* Munich: DTV, 1965. English translation: *Goebbels*. Boston: Da Capo, 1983.

Herbst, Ludolf. *Hitlers Charisma. Die Erfindung eines deutschen Messias.* Frankfurt am Main: Fischer, 2010.

Heuss, Theodor. *Hitlers Weg. Eine historisch-politische Studie über den Nationalsozialismus*. Stuttgart, Berlin, Leipzig: Union, 1932.

Heydecker, Joe and Johannes Leeb. *Der Nürnberger Prozeß*. Cologne: Kiepenheuer and Witsch 1979. English translation: *The Nuremberg Trial.* London: Heinemann, 1962.

Hilberg, Raul. *Die Vernichtung der europäischen Juden*. 3 volumes. Frankfurt am Main: Fischer, 1990. English original: *The Destruction of the European Jews*. 3 volumes. New Haven: Yale University Press, 1961.

Huttner, Markus. *Totalitarismus und säkulare Religionen. Zur Frühgeschichte totalitarismuskritischer Begriffs- und Theoriebildung in Großbritannien.* Bonn: Bouvier, 1999.

Jäckel, Eberhard. *Hitlers Weltanschauung. Entwurf einer Herrschaft*. Revised and expanded ed. Stuttgart: DVA, 1981. English translation: *Hitler's Weltanschauung.* Middletown, Connecticut: Wesleyan Press, 1972.

Kershaw, lan. *Hitler*. 2 volumes. *Vol 1: 1889–1936.* Stuttgart: DVA, 1998; *Vol. 2. 1936–1945.* Stuttgart: DVA, 2000. English original: *Hitler 1889–1936: Hubris.* London: Allen Lane, 1998; *Hitler 1936–1945: Nemesis*. London: Allen Lane, 2000.

Kopper, Joachim. *Die Metaphysik Meister Eckharts.* Saarbrücken: West-Ost-Verlag, 1955.

Ley, Michael. *Genozid und Heilserwartung. Zum nationalsozialistischen Mord am europäischen Judentum.* Vienna: Picus Verlag, 1993.

Ley, Michael and Julius H. Schoeps, eds. *Der Nationalsozialismus als politische Religion*. Bodenheim bei Mainz: Philo Verlags Gesellschaft, 1997.

Ley, Michael. Heinrich Neisser, Gilbert Weiss, eds. *Politische Religion? Politik, Religion und Anthropologie im Werk von Eric Voegelin*. Munich: Fink, 2003.

Lifton, Robert Jay. *Revolutionary Immortality: Mao Tse-Tung and the Chinese Cultural Revolution*. London: Weidenfels and Nicolson, 1968.

Linse, Ulrich. *Barfüßige Propheten. Erlöser der zwanziger Jahre*. Berlin: Siedler Verlag, 1983.

Longerich, Peter. *Heinrich Himmler. Biographie.* Munich: Siedler Verlag, 2008. English translation: *Heinrich Himmler: A Life.* Oxford: Oxford University Press, 2011.

Longerich, Peter. *Goebbels. Biographie.* Munich: Siedler Verlag, 2010. English translation: *Goebbels.* New York: Random House, 2015.

Lübbe, Hermann. *Heilserwartung und Terror. Politische Religionen des 20. Jahrhunderts.* Düsseldorf: Patmos Verlag, 1995.

Maier, Hans and Michael Schäfer, eds. *Totalitarismus und politische Religionen. Konzepte des Diktaturvergleichs: Vol. 2*. Paderborn: Schöningh, 1997. English translation: *Totalitarianism and Political Religions, Vol. 2: Concepts for the Comparison of Dictatorships (Totalitarian Movements and Political Religions).* London: Routledge, 2012.

Maier, Hans, ed. *Totalitarismus und politische Religionen. Konzepte des Diktaturvergleichs*. Paderborn: Schöningh, 1996. English translation: *Totalitarianism and Political Religions, Vol. 1: Concepts for the Comparison of Dictatorships (Totalitarian Movements and Political Religions).* London: Routledge, 2005.

——. *Totalitarismus und politische Religionen. Vol. 3: Deutungsgeschichte und Theorie.* Paderborn, 2003. English translation: *Totalitarianism and Political Religions, Vol. 3: Concepts for the Comparison of Dictatorships. Theory and History of Interpretations (Totalitarianism Movements and Political Religions)*. London: Routledge, 2012.

Mosse, George L. *Die Nationalisierung der Massen. Von den Befreiungskriegen bis zum Dritten Reich.* Frankfurt am Main and Berlin: Ullstein, 1976. English original: *The Nationalization of the Masses: Political Symbolism and Mass Movements in Germany, from the Napoleonic Wars Through the Third Reich*. New York: H. Fertig, 1975.

Münkler, Herfried. *Die Deutschen und ihre Mythen.* Rowohlt: Berlin, 2009.

Murawski, Erich. *Der deutsche Wehrmachtsbericht 1939–1945. Ein Beitrag zur Untersuchung der geistigen Kriegsführung.* Boppard: Boldt, 1962.

Nagel, Alexander K., Bernd U. Schipper, Ansgar Weymann, eds. *Apokalypse. Zur Soziologie und Geschichte religiöser Krisenrhetorik.* Frankfurt am Main: Campus Verlag, 2008.

Neumann, Sigmund. *Permanent Revolution: The Total State in a World at War*. New York : Harper Brothers, 1942.

Piper, Ernst. *Alfred Rosenberg: Hitlers Chefideologe.* Munich: Blessing, 2005.

Puschner, Uwe. *Die völkische Bewegung im wilhelminischen Kaiserreich. Sprache — Rasse — Religion.* Darmstadt: Wiss. Buchgesellschaft, 2001.

Puschner, Uwe and Clemens Vollnhals, eds. *Die völkisch-religiöse Bewegung im Nationalsozialismus. Eine Beziehungs und Konfliktgeschichte.* Göttingen: Vandenhoek and Ruprecht, 2012.

Reemtsma, Jan Philipp. *Vertrauen und Gewalt. Versuch über eine besondere Konstellation der Moderne*. Hamburg: Hamburger Edition, 2009. English translation: *Trust and Violence*. Princeton: Princeton University Press, 2012.

Reichel, Peter. *Der schöne Schein des Dritten Reiches. Faszination und Gewalt des Faschismus.* Frankfurt am Main: Fischer Taschenbuch Verlag, 1993.

Reuth, Ralf Georg. *Goebbels.* Munich: Piper, 1990. English translation: *Goebbels.* New York: Harcourt, 1993.

De Rougemont, Denis. *Journal d'Allemagne.* Paris: Gallimard, 1938; German translation : *Journal aus Deutschland 1935–1936.* Berlin: Aufbau Verlag, 2001.

Safranski, Rüdiger. *Das Böse oder Das Drama der Freiheit.* Munich and Vienna: Hanser, 1997.

Schmeer, Karlheinz. *Die Regie des öffentlichen Lebens im Dritten Reich*. Munich: Pohl, 1956.

Carl Schmitt. *Politische Theologie. Vier Kapitel zur Lehre von der Souveränität*. 3rd ed. Berlin: Duncker and Humblot, 1979. English translation: *Political Theology. Four Chapters on the Concept of Sovereignty*. Translated by George Schwab. Cambridge, Massachusetts: MIT Press, 1985.

Schnurbein, Stefanie V., and Justus H. Ulbricht, eds. *Völkische Religion und Krisen der Moderne. Entwürfe 'arteigener' Glaubenssysteme seit der Jahrhundertwende.* Würzburg: Königshausen and Neumann, 2001.

Scholder, Klaus. *Die Kirchen und das Dritte Reich*. 3 volumes. Frankfurt am Main: Propyläen, 1977–2001. English translation: *The Churches and the Third Reich, Vol. 1.* London: Hymns Ancient and Modern Ltd., 2012. *Vol. 2.* Philadelphia: Fortress Press, 1988.

Sémelin, Jacques. *Säubern und Vernichten. Die Politik der Massaker und Völkermorde.* Hamburg: Hamburg Edition, 2007. English translation (of the French original): *Purify and Destroy: The Political Uses of Massacre and Genocide.* New York: Columbia University Press, 2009.

Sironneau, Jean-Pierre. *Sécularisation et religions politiques.* La Haye, Paris, New York: Mouton, 1982.

Snyder, Timothy. *Bloodlands. Europa zwischen Hitler und Stalin*. 3rd ed. Munich: Beck, 2011. English original: *Bloodlands: Europe Between Hitler and Stalin.* New York: Basic Books, 2010.

Sofsky, Wolfgang. *Traktat über die Gewalt*. Frankfurt am Main: Fischer, 1996.

Speer, Albert. *Erinnerungen.* Berlin: Propylaen, 1969. English translation. *Inside The Third Reich: Memoires*. New York: MacMillan, 1969.

Steineck, Christian. *Grundstrukturen mystischen Denkens.* Würzburg: Königshausen and Neumann, 2000.

Strohm, Christoph. *Die Kirchen im Dritten Reich.* Munich: Beck, 2011.

Thamer, Hans-Ulrich. *Verführung und Gewalt. Deutschland 1933–1945.* Berlin: Siedler, 1998.

Thamer, Hans-Ulrich, Simone Erpel, *Hitler und die Deutschen. Volksgemeinschaft und Verbrechen* (Ausstellungskatalog). Dresden: Deutsches Historisches Museum, 2010.

Trimondi, Victor and Victoria Trimondi. *Krieg der Religionen. Politik, Glaube und Terror im Zeichen der Apokalypse.* Munich: Fink, 2006.

Voegelin, Eric. *Rasse und Staat*. Tübingen: J. C. B. Mohr [Paul Siebeck], 1933. English translation: *Race and State, The Collected Works of Eric Voegelin, Vol. 2*, edited with an Introduction by Klaus Vondung. Baton Rouge: Louisiana State University Press, 1997.

———. *Die politischen Religionen*. Series "Ausblicke." Vienna: Bermann-Fischer, 1938; 2nd ed. Stockholm, 1939. Reprint of 2nd ed. edited by Peter J. Opitz. Munich: Fink, 1993. English translation: *The Political Religions, The Collected Works of Eric Voegelin, Vol. 5: Modernity Without Restraint*. Edited with an Introduction by Manfred Henningsen. Columbia: University of Missouri Press, 2000.

Vondung, Klaus. *Magie und Manipulation. Ideologischer Kult und politische Religion des Nationalsozialismus*. Göttingen: Vandenhoeck and Ruprecht, 1971.

———. *Die Apokalypse in Deutschland*. Munich: DTV, 1988. English translation: *The Apocalypse in Germany*. Columbia: University of Missouri Press, 2000.

Waldschütz, Erwin. *Denken und Erfahren des Grundes. Zur philosophischen Deutung Meister Eckharts*. Vienna: Herder, 1989.

Wehler, Hans-Ulrich. *Der Nationalsozialismus: Bewegung, Führerherrschaft, Verbrechen. 1919–1945*. Munich: Beck, 2009.

ABBREVIATIONS

BDM	Bund Deutscher Mädel in der Hitler-Jugend [League of German Girls within the Hitler Youth]
DAF	Deutsche Arbeitsfront [German Labor Front]
DnG	Die neue Gemeinschaft. [The New Community] An internal periodical that provided guidelines for the establishment and celebration of ceremonies and other holiday events.
HA	Hauptamt [Central Office]
HJ	Hitler-Jugend [Hitler Youth]
HWPh	Historisches Wörterbuch der Philosophie. 13 vols. Darmstadt: Wiss. Buchgesellschaft 1971–2007.
IfZ	Institut für Zeitgeschichte, Munich [Institute of Contemporary History]
KdF	NS-Gemeinschaft "Kraft durch Freude" in der Deutschen Arbeitsfront [National Socialist Community "Strength through Joy" within the German Labor Front]
LThK	*Lexikon für Theologie und Kirche*. 11 vols. 3rd. rev. ed. Freiburg: Herder, 1993–2001.

MA	Mikrofilmarchiv im Institut für Zeitgeschichte, München (Archivsignatur) [Microfilm Archive of the Institute of Contemporary History in Munich]
MadR	Meldungen aus dem Reich [Reports from the Reich]
NS	Nationalsozialismus or nationalsozialistisch [National Socialism, national socialist]
NSDAP	Nationalsozialistische Deutsche Arbeiterpartei [National Socialist German Workers' Party]
NSDStB	Nationalsozialistischer Deutscher Studentenbund [National Socialist German Students' League]
NSLB	Nationalsozialistischer Lehrerbund [National Socialist Teachers' League]
OSAF	Oberste SA-Führung [Supreme Command of the SA]
RAD	Reichsarbeitsdienst [Reich Labor Service]
RFSS	Reichsführung-SS bzw. Reichsführer-SS und Chef der deutschen Polizei [Reichleadership-SS, Reichfuehrer-SS and Head of the German Police]
RGG	*Die Religion in Geschichte und Gegenwart. Handwörterbuch für Theologie und Religionswissenschaft*. 6 vols. 3rd ed. Tübingen: Mohr Siebeck, 1957–1962. Also, 4th ed. completely revised in 8 vols. with an index volume. Tübingen: Mohr Siebeck, 1998–2007.

RJF	Reichsjugendführung [National Youth Leadership]
RPL	Reichspropagandaleitung [Reich's Propaganda Directorate]
RSHA	Reichssicherheitshauptamt [Main security office of the German state.]
SA	Sturmabteilung [Storm Section]
SD	Sicherheitsdienst [Security Service]
SD-B	SD-Berichte zu Inlandsfragen [SD Reports on Domestic Matters]
SS	Schutzstaffel [Defense (or Protection) Squadron]
VB	Völkischer Beobachter [The Peoples' Observer]
VOBl. NSDAP	Verordnungsblatt der NSDAP [Official Gazette of the NSDAP]
Vorschläge	*Vorschläge der Reichspropagandaleitung zur nationalsozialistischen Feiergestaltung*. Nur für Dienststellen der Partei bestimmt. Gesamtverantwortlich. Fritz Kaiser: Munich, 1935–36 [Suggestions of the Reich's Propaganda Directorate for planning and organizing celebrations and ceremonies. For the exclusive use of Party offices.]
ZfDW	Zeitschrift für Deutsche Wortforschung [Journal for German Linguistic Research]

INDEX OF PHOTOGRAPHS

Introduction: HJ and BDM at the Reich Party Congress 1938. Photo: *Der Parteitag Großdeutschland* ed. by Hanns Kerrl (Berlin: Weller, 1939).

1. Political Religion?: Reich Party Congress in Nuremberg 1934. Roll call of the SA and SS in the Luitpold Arena. Honoring the fallen heroes. Bundesarchiv Bild I02-04062A/CC-BY-SA.

2. Faith: Adolf Hitler's 48th birthday. Berlin, April 20, 1937. Photo: Bildagentur für Kunst, Kultur und Geschichte, 30027927.

3. Mysticism: Reich Party Congress in Nuremberg 1937. Roll call of the political leaders on the Zeppelin field. "Dome of light". Photo: *Der Parteitag der Arbeit vom 6. bis 13.September 1937* (Munich: Eher, 1938).

4. Myth and Ritual: Memorial March to the Feldherrnhalle on November 9, 1936. Photo: Bayerisches Hauptstaatsarchiv, Bildersammlung 3123.

5. Cult: Hitler consecrates the new banners with the "Blutfahne" at the Reich Party Congress 1938. Photo: Reich Party Congress in Nuremberg 1938. *Der Parteitag Großdeutschland* ed. by Hanns Kerrl (Berlin: Weller, 1939).

6. Theology: At a ceremony on May 1, 1933 the University of Hamburg confesses its faith in the "National Revolution" and in Adolf Hitler. Photo: Hamburger Bibliothek für Universitätsgeschichte.

7. Apocalypse: The "ramp" at concentration camp Auschwitz II — Birkenau. Photo of SS-Hauptscharführer Bernhard Walter during the arrival of Hungarian Jews in May 1944; *Sterbebücher von Auschwitz*, Vol. 1. Berichte ed. by the Staatl. Museum Auschwitz-Birkenau (Munich et. al.: Saur, 1995).

INDEX

NOTE ON THE AUTHOR

Klaus Vondung is Professor Emeritus in German Studies at the University of Siegen, Germany. His research and teaching abroad include a Visiting Scholarship at the Hoover Institution, Stanford University, and Visiting Professorships at the University of Florida, Gainesville, the University of Houston, Kansai University, Suita/Osaka, and KwanseiGakuin University, Nishinomiya. He is permanent Honorary Guest Professor at Zhejiang University, Hangzhou. In addition to numerous books and articles in German, in English he has published the book *The Apocalypse in Germany* (2000), edited *Race and State* and *The History of the Race Idea* in *The Collected Works of Eric Voegelin*, and is the author of many articles in journals and essay volumes.

NOTE ON THE TRANSLATOR

Dr. William Petropulos, formally research fellow at the Eric-Voegelin Archive of the Ludwig-Maximilians-Universität München, was co-editor and English translator for two volumes of *The Collected Works of Eric Voegelin*, and translator for two further volumes. In addition to translating numerous articles for academic journals in the areas of Political Theory and the History of Ideas, he is also the translator of *A Friendship That Lasted A Lifetime: The Correspondence Between Alfred Schütz and Eric Voegelin*, edited by Gerhard Wagner and Gilbert Weiss.